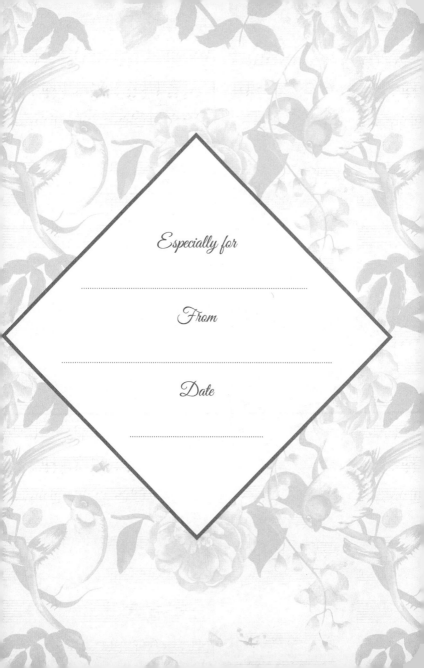

Especially for

....

From

....

Date

....

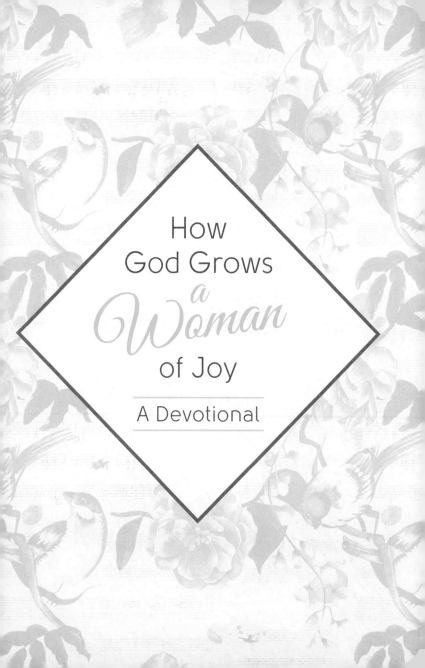

How
God Grows
a
Woman
of Joy

A Devotional

Anita Higman

How God Grows a *Woman* of Joy

A Devotional

BARBOUR BOOKS
An Imprint of Barbour Publishing, Inc.

Print ISBN 978-1-64352-202-9

eBook Editions:
Adobe Digital Edition (.epub) 978-1-64352-397-2
Kindle and MobiPocket Edition (.prc) 978-1-64352-398-9

Published by Barbour Books, an imprint of Barbour Publishing, Inc., 1810 Barbour Drive, Uhrichsville, Ohio 44683, www.barbourbooks.com

Our mission is to inspire the world with the life-changing message of the Bible.

Member of the
Evangelical Christian
Publishers Association

Printed in China.

Dedication

To Shannon Perry
God has given this world many blessings,
and you are one of them, my friend.
Thank you for shining the light and love
and joy of Christ wherever you go!

Anita Higman

Introduction

Joy—such a little word to hold such a big emotion! Sometimes that sensation of pleasure or happiness seems impossible to obtain though—as if it is a jar of pretty feelings placed so high on a shelf that even Christians can't quite reach it. Yes, this life can be hard, and even Jesus said there would be trouble in our earthly journey. Yet in spite of our fallen world and these frail vessels of ours, the Lord's Word is full of assurances that He will fill us with joy. And He alone has the supernatural power to make good on those promises. May we discover, celebrate, and share this little-big word called *joy*!

A Sense of Wonder

"I was there. . .when he gave the sea its boundary so the waters would not overstep his command, and when he marked out the foundations of the earth. Then I was constantly at his side. I was filled with delight day after day, rejoicing always in his presence, rejoicing in his whole world and delighting in mankind."
PROVERBS 8:27, 29–31 NIV

Your child squats on the seashore to investigate a shell. You think it's nice, but since you have too many at home, you secretly hope he will toss it back. But your boy is an explorer extraordinaire, and well, he thinks that shell looks like a spaceship. As he makes noises that scare away the wildlife nearby, he is a boy no longer. He's a superhero with a red cape, and he is out to foil the dark plot of the aliens before they destroy the universe!

And here you thought it was just a shell. . . .

Yes, kids can be full of the sillies, and yet their play is valuable. They learn. They grow. They cherish a sense of delight and wonder over all that God has created.

Then there on the beach, your boy falls exhausted onto your lap and whispers, "I did it, Mom. I saved you from the aliens. . . because I love you."

Then you decide that shell is one of the best treasures ever found.

Lord, may I always take joy in my child's delight, and may I continue to hold on to my sense of wonder. Amen.

The Worst Kind of Thief

Be sober-minded; be watchful. Your adversary the devil prowls around like a roaring lion, seeking someone to devour.
1 PETER 5:8 ESV

You sit in a heap on the floor—drowning in confusion and anger and fear, traumatized from what you found when you came home from work. Someone broke into your home and stole your most prized possessions—family heirlooms, like your mother's wedding ring and your granny's handmade quilt. And while the invader tore around your home looking for valuables, he managed to leave a gargantuan mess from all his tearing and soiling and breaking things. What to do? You call the police so they can find the thief and deliver justice.

The devil is the worst kind of thief, deceiver, and destroyer. He will try very hard to come in and take away all that you treasure—joy, peace, love—and leave you in a wake of confusion and anger and fear. So, may we always be sober-minded. May we be watchful. Call on the Lord any time of the day or night. Rely on His perfect hand of justice, His tender mercies, and His mighty power to restore!

Lord, thank You that I can call on You day or night whenever I feel the enemy is trying to deceive me or destroy me. Amen.

Delight Yourself in the Lord!

Trust in the LORD, and do good; dwell in the land and befriend faithfulness. Delight yourself in the LORD, and he will give you the desires of your heart. Commit your way to the LORD; trust in him, and he will act.

PSALM 37:3–5 ESV

Name a few things that bring you delight. Is it the whiskery twitch of a bunny's nose? Is it the pure crisp mist on an alpine slope? Perhaps the happy toast to the bride and groom? Or you might also find delight in the forgiveness between friends. The rocking lullabies sung to your newborn babe. The morning praises to God on a bright new day. Or maybe the chat you had with the Lord on your long drive to work. All good and lovely things for you and the Lord to enjoy together.

When you stay heart-close to the Lord, you wouldn't want to do anything to mar that friendship. So you will delight in the same things. You will delight in each other.

That's the way it goes with good friends.

Oh Lord, I thank You that You are my dearest and closest friend. Be ever near me, and may we delight in the company of each other. So much so that when I rise up to be with You for eternity, I will already know You well! Amen.

Feeling Wild and Weary?

And rising very early in the morning, while it
was still dark, he departed and went out to
a desolate place, and there he prayed.
MARK 1:35 ESV

You've gotten yourself so wearied and wild-eyed with life that you can't fall asleep at night. You can't concentrate. You can't do much of anything but thrash around while your head is screaming, "What is wrong with me? I feel like some dying star that is about to implode!" Right now, you can't even imagine a restful and focused life, let alone a life filled with joy.

You could always ask yourself, "Have I spent any time with God in prayer? Do I relax in the Lord's company, His sweet fellowship, His gentle corrections and challenges? His guidance and wisdom and refreshment?" As scripture reminds us, even Christ showed us how essential prayer was while He was on this earth.

There is indeed a cure for all who feel wild and weary. God is waiting.

Lord, I admit I get wrapped up tighter and tighter in
the wearisome ways of the world, and it has made me sick
in body and mind and spirit. Please help me never to see
our time together as "just another thing on my to-do list,"
but as precious fellowship with my dearest friend. Amen.

A Holy Ornament

*But like the Holy One who called you, be holy yourselves
in all your conduct [be set apart from the world by
your godly character and moral courage].*
1 PETER 1:15 AMP

Oh my. The Christmas tree turned out better this year than ever before. It's absolutely resplendent. Radiant ornaments of every shape and size glow and sparkle before you. You just can't take your eyes from the beauty of it all. It makes you want to walk up and take a closer look, to sigh with joy and then share your festive tree with others!

As Christians we can be holy ornaments for God. What an opportunity. What a divine calling. May our character be so godly and our conduct so holy that the world can't take their eyes off the luminous wonder they see in us. So much so that the world will choose to take a closer look. Their souls will sigh, and then hopefully, they will ask a most important question. "Where does your light come from?"

May our joy and our love and our truth shine—absolutely resplendent—not just at Christmastime but all year long!

*Holy Spirit, show me how to shine Your divine light
like a holy ornament in this dark world. Amen.*

A Promise for All Seasons

"For I know the plans I have for you, declares the LORD, plans for welfare and not for evil, to give you a future and a hope."
JEREMIAH 29:11 ESV

The older we get, the more we realize that life can have an ebb and flow like the sea. Of losses and gains, of joys and sorrows. Of laughter and tears. Of wellness and illness. Of hellos and goodbyes. These passages have parallels to the changes we witness every year in nature. There are days of summery pleasures and busy tasks. We see autumn moments of calm reflection and satisfying contentment. We come to know the bleak winter episodes of trials, grief, fear, and loneliness as well as the many occasions of springtime growth and vitality when our spirits rise with renewed hope. No matter where we are in life, we can find joy in knowing that the Bible is full of promises from God.

One of the many assurances from the Lord is in Philippians 4:19 (NLT): "And this same God who takes care of me will supply all your needs from his glorious riches, which have been given to us in Christ Jesus."

Take heart. God loves you. God will supply your needs from His glorious riches. And that, my friend, is a promise for all seasons!

Dearest Lord, thank You for supplying all my needs through the ebb and flow of life. Amen.

The Heavenly Scent of Forgiveness

Bearing with one another and, if one has a complaint
against another, forgiving each other; as the Lord
has forgiven you, so you also must forgive.
COLOSSIANS 3:13 ESV

In a bygone era, people would always hang up their sheets on a clothesline to dry in the breeze. Later when you gathered them down in your arms, ohhh, they smelled so fresh and clean and sun-drenched. No fabric softener ever came close to that heavenly scent. People love things that are clean and fresh. Why wouldn't they? Somewhere deep down it strikes a chord, reminding us of that glorious state of our souls before the fall.

Because of the work of Christ on the cross, we can know that clean and fragrant scent of forgiveness. No other method of heart cleansing—that the world endorses—can ever compare. To forgive in the name of Christ and to be forgiven by our Lord satisfies in ways far beyond the senses, since it is a true cleansing of the spirit.

Yes, yes, that is what we need. So, is there someone you need to forgive today? When you do, bask in that washed-clean feeling and let it drench you in joy!

Precious Lord Jesus, I forgive _____
for what she did. Thank You for all the times
You've so generously forgiven me! Amen.

Joy in Correction?

Better is an open reprimand [of loving correction] than love that is hidden. Faithful are the wounds of a friend [who corrects out of love and concern], but the kisses of an enemy are deceitful [because they serve his hidden agenda].
PROVERBS 27:5–6 AMP

Mmm, mmm. Your friend sure does love life. She sure does love people. And boy, does she love to talk! But sometimes that mountain of yak contains a few scoops of gossip. You've witnessed it one too many times, but you hate to be the one who brings it up. And yet, you've read that verse in Proverbs 27. What to do?

Ask the Holy Spirit for the best way to approach the situation. What to say and when to say it. Hopefully, she will come to see that reproof from a faithful friend can be helpful, while the gushing praises of an enemy are deceiving.

But then, of course, correction works both ways. If a Christian friend comes to you with a gentle rebuke, pray about it, and then do whatever the Lord asks you to do. Perhaps you too will come to benefit from the growth and joy of a benevolent rebuke!

Lord, help me to accept loving corrections. With all my heart I want to grow into a mature Christian woman! Amen.

We Are That Sweet Perfume!

*But thanks be to God, who in Christ always leads us
in triumphal procession, and through us spreads the
fragrance of the knowledge of him everywhere. For we
are the aroma of Christ to God among those who are
being saved and among those who are perishing, to one a
fragrance from death to death, to the other a fragrance
from life to life. Who is sufficient for these things?*
2 CORINTHIANS 2:14–16 ESV

She is nearly sprinting through the mall—obviously a woman on a mission—but no matter how busy she is, she can't help but pause at one of the many perfume counters. Why? Maybe because she loves to breathe in a scent that draws her back to some wonderful memories of a beloved family member. Or she wants to take in an essence that her senses have never encountered before. Something winsome and beautiful and irresistible.

As Christians we are to be that winsome and beautiful and irresistible fragrance of Christ—and no matter how busy people are, hopefully they will want to pause as we share His love, His truth, and His life.

*Mighty God, everywhere I go, may I be part of the
triumphal procession that spreads the fragrance of the
knowledge of Your Son. In Jesus' name I pray, amen.*

Do You Have a Nickname?

James son of Zebedee and his brother John (to them he gave the name Boanerges, which means "sons of thunder").
MARK 3:17 NIV

Most people love nicknames. Well, that is, if the name is meant to portray something endearing. Like Sweetness and Light or Lambkin or Sugar Plum. Then there are the nicknames that might not be as adorable, such as Stinky, Muffinhead, or Goobers. In fact, they make us wince.

There is some debate among biblical scholars about why Jesus nicknamed James and John the "Sons of Thunder." Could it have been their sometimes impetuous and blustery nature? Their noise levels when they were together? Or perhaps it was for another reason? We may never know, but it is fascinating that even Jesus used nicknames.

So, it might be interesting to ponder these questions. If the Lord gave *you* a nickname, what might it be? If you could distill the essence of your character into several key words—or if your friends did that task for you—what might that list look like? Does your daily walk reflect the hope and light and love and joy of Christ? If Jesus were indeed to give you a nickname, what would you *want* it to be?

Lord, I want to please You in every way. Help me to be a woman of godly substance. I want to make You proud! Amen.

Finding Your Joy Again

Whoever oppresses the poor shows contempt for their Maker, but whoever is kind to the needy honors God.
PROVERBS 14:31 NIV

Lately life has been as mean as a junkyard dog—and it's been busy trying to rip and tear a sizable hole in your soul. You are struggling with problems you never even saw coming. Truth be told, you have run out of good sleep. You have run out of steam. And you for sure have run out of smiles.

One activity that can bring back some of that joy is to turn some of your focus to the needs of others. One of the places that will generally welcome some help is the local food pantry. Stop by and ask how you can assist them. Many times they are running low on some of the basic nonperishables. Make a list of the items they need, do the shopping, and then donate those food supplies as a gift. With this benevolent deed you are not only being kind to the poor, but according to Proverbs 14:31, you are also honoring God. This biblical assurance warms the heart and touches the soul, and it will also help bring back your joy.

Lord, please give me a heart for the needy. Show me the many ways I can be compassionate and generous. Amen.

A Gathering of Goodies

The world of the generous gets larger and larger; the world of the stingy gets smaller and smaller. The one who blesses others is abundantly blessed; those who help others are helped.

PROVERBS 11:24–25 MSG

People love accumulating things. A little more of this. A little more of that. People could make lyrics to it and sing it to the tune of "Here We Come A-wassailing." Only it would be "Here we go a-gathering. . .la-la, la-la, la-la. . ."

But as we enjoy the glories of a-gathering, wouldn't it be nice if we could also enjoy a-sharing? You know, like giving away some of those wonderful goodies in your pantry. Or maybe a few of the slightly worn clothes from your closet. Or perhaps you could donate some of the cash you intended to use for those nonsensical items that always turn out to be a waste of money. Or maybe you could even offer the use of your home for a Bible study.

There are any number of ways to be generous with what God has so graciously given us. And we will find that this sharing will make our world larger and larger. Granted, the blessings that come back to us might not always be material possessions. It might just be good old-fashioned joy. But who couldn't use more of that commodity, eh?

Lord, transform me into a bighearted soul who loves a-sharing as much as a-gathering. Amen.

You Are Not Alone

*Have mercy on me, LORD, for I am in distress. Tears blur
my eyes. My body and soul are withering away.*
PSALM 31:9 NLT

The dear woman dropped on the couch in utter exhaustion,
her heart broken into too many pieces to count—perhaps even
too many to ever be mended. She had cried until her heart was
pounding and her eyes were nearly swollen shut. Life had done
its worst and then some.

If that woman is you, you are not alone. Through the centuries,
people have known every manner of trouble and travail. You can
see it over and over in the Bible, and in many instances those
lamenting passages are in the book of Psalms.

But also in the same book are the assurances of supernatural
help such as Psalm 94:16–19 (MSG): "Who stood up for me against
the wicked? Who took my side against evil workers? If GOD hadn't
been there for me, I never would have made it. The minute I said,
'I'm slipping, I'm falling,' your love, GOD, took hold and held me
fast. When I was upset and beside myself, you calmed me down
and cheered me up."

*Holy Spirit, show me the path to joy, but when
trials do come, please use the times of trouble
for my growth and Your glory. Amen.*

What Are Your Joy Makers?

Come, let's shout praises to GOD, raise the roof for the Rock who saved us! Let's march into his presence singing praises, lifting the rafters with our hymns!
PSALM 95:1–2 MSG

Do you have a list of things that bring you joy? Is it a leisurely stroll, beachcombing for pretty shell treasures along a sandy shore? Is it freshly brewed coffee and laughter with a friend at a local café? Is it cozying up by a fire and reading a page-turning novel with your favorite characters?

And when it comes to your devotions, isn't it pure joy to have an especially wondrous time with the Lord in the quietude of a solitary place? How about adding music to the glory of those moments as it suggests in the Psalms? Even if your voice is more of a croak than a croon, you can still make a joyful noise unto the Lord. He is worthy of that praise, and He will delight in your heart songs. Soon you will want to add those melodious tributes to your list of joy makers!

Lord Jesus, I want to come into Your presence daily, worshipping You in every way, even with shouts of joy and songs of praise. May my praise bring us both delight! Amen.

Freedom Will Be Glorious

No temptation has overtaken you that is not common to man. God is faithful, and he will not let you be tempted beyond your ability, but with the temptation he will also provide the way of escape, that you may be able to endure it. Therefore, my beloved, flee from idolatry.
1 CORINTHIANS 10:13–14 ESV

Since merely being alive on this earth can be perilous, it's easy to get sucked into addictions. We feel justified. The immediate gratification seems almost vital, as well as a protective buffer against the harshness of reality. But what can at first seem like a friend can soon become a fiend when we aren't paying attention. These dependencies come in many forms. There are the obvious dark indulgences like illegal drugs, porn, and gambling, but even good things can become a bad habit if not kept in check, such as TV, social media, shopping, gaming, desserts, our phones, and a host of other gadgets and goodies that keep us so busy we forget how to live—really live the way God intended.

So what do you do when you find yourself wasting your life away with an addiction? Flee to God. He is faithful to provide a way of escape. Ask Him to show you the life He intended for you. Life will be full. Freedom will be glorious.

Merciful God, show me any addictions I might have and please release me from them! In Jesus' name I pray, amen.

Bad Case of the What-Ifs

Trust in the LORD with all your heart, and do not lean on your own understanding. In all your ways acknowledge him, and he will make straight your paths.

It's midnight and you've come down with something far worse than a cold. You have a bad case of the what-ifs. What if your boss uses your ideas in the meeting and doesn't give you credit? What if your water heater goes kerflooey right after the warranty is up? What if you get seriously ill and your insurance doesn't pay for all the doctor visits? What if you marry a man who's unfaithful? What if your friends abandon you, or your children grow to hate you? Yeah, those kinds of sinister mind games can go on all night.

Thank God we can turn to Him when we fear the future. When bad times come and they don't seem to want to go away. We are not to trust in our own frail understanding of the way life works. But if we trust God completely, He will make our paths straight. The Lord may not take away every trial, but He promises to be with us through every spiritual battle, every hardship. With God involved in our lives, it's not just a way to make do. It's a way to have nights of good sleep and days of real joy.

Lord, please show me how to trust You with every detail of my life. Amen.

When You Butt Heads

Be humble and gentle. Be patient with each other, making allowance for each other's faults because of your love.
EPHESIANS 4:2 TLB

Have you ever watched bighorn sheep come together in a battle, bashing into each other with thundering force? Each strike is as alarming as it is awesome.

Everyone has somebody they butt heads with. A coworker who enjoys those backhanded compliments at your expense, or a family member who never appreciates you, or maybe even a church friend who takes advantage of you. It is inevitable that you won't get along perfectly with everyone, and if you and the other person tend to have strong-willed personalities, well, out come the bighorn sheep for some bashing. And it won't be an awesome sight.

As Christians, how does God want us to deal with headstrong people? The same way He expects us to live and work and play with everyone. We will need humbleness and gentleness and patience. Sound hopeless? It is. Utterly.

But nothing is impossible with God. Only His transformative power can change the temperament of a bighorn sheep into a gentle lamb. And then you will find that joy, sweet joy, will come more easily.

Lord, I have a really hard time with _____.
Please show me how to love her as You would.
And help me not to be so pigheaded too! Amen.

If Only

*Not that I am speaking of being in need, for I have
learned in whatever situation I am to be content.*
PHILIPPIANS 4:11 ESV

Have you ever thought, *Happiness would be mine. . .if only*? What
if all your prayers were answered just the way you want them?
Hmm. First, you might ask God for a full-body healing. Oh, and
kids who obey you and sing your praises. A husband who loves
you and remembers your birthday. A satisfying job where you're
paid a great deal of cash! The perfect church. A big house in a
fine neighborhood and lots of loyal friends who make you laugh.
Okay, so once you have all of that, you'd want the same blessings for all your family—oh, and all your friends. But you wouldn't
stop there. Soon you would see that the entire world would
need the same help.

In other words, you want heaven. But this fallen earth isn't
heaven. So while we wait for heaven, what can we do? Pray like
we mean it. Be thankful for answered prayers and the blessings
that do come. And never get so caught up in the "if onlys" that
we waste our lives away waiting for a perfect life. May we learn
to find joy in the present and, like Paul, learn to be content in all
circumstances.

*Lord, I don't want to get so caught up wanting heaven on
earth now that I forget to find joy with You every day. Amen.*

Throw Open That Door!

*If we claim that we're free of sin, we're only fooling ourselves.
A claim like that is errant nonsense. On the other hand,
if we admit our sins—make a clean breast of them—he won't
let us down; he'll be true to himself. He'll forgive our sins
and purge us of all wrongdoing. If we claim that we've never
sinned, we out-and-out contradict God—make a liar out of
him. A claim like that only shows off our ignorance of God.*
1 John 1:8–10 MSG

Your grandmother had a name for it—she called it Fibber McGee's closet. It's when there is way too much junk crammed into a closet so that when you open it, all the stuff tumbles out onto the floor.

We sometimes try very cleverly to hide our sins from God— kind of like Fibber McGee's closet—but eventually it will all come tumbling out. If we keep telling ourselves that we are sin-free, we are lying to ourselves. We just need to come clean. God knows what's inside anyway. So let's open those jam-packed closets and let the Lord's light shine inside. We will find forgiveness and peace there. And such joy!

*Lord, please forgive me for _____. I humbly repent.
Show me how to avoid that transgression in the future. Amen.*

Discernment

The Pharisee was astonished to see that he did not first wash before dinner. And the Lord said to him, "Now you Pharisees cleanse the outside of the cup and of the dish, but inside you are full of greed and wickedness. You fools! Did not he who made the outside make the inside also?"
LUKE 11:38–40 ESV

When you were a kid, did you hear your mom say, "No, you can't," or "Don't even think about it"? We get the impression from an early age that there's a lot of stuff out there—some dangerous, yes, but some joy filled—that people shake their heads at. We rediscover this later in life and sometimes even in church. Yes, we need to always follow the Ten Commandments and the Lord's precepts in the Bible, but when the church sets up a separate system of strict rules to follow, it's time to listen to God—not man. Jesus wasn't a fan of the legalistic Pharisees. In fact, He called them fools when they cared more about being clean on the outside than on the inside.

Today's legalisms might imply, "I don't trust Christ's grace. I'll add a list of rules to secure my salvation." Legalisms can keep us so busy there's little time for a relationship with Christ. Legalisms diminish the personal while they elevate the prideful. Be wary of such devious ploys. Satan is an enemy to truth and to joy.

Holy Spirit, please give me a discerning heart. Amen.

I Can't Live without You!

*"Look! I stand at the door and knock. If you hear
my voice and open the door, I will come in,
and we will share a meal together as friends."*
REVELATION 3:20 NLT

Maybe you've told a friend, "Here's a summary of my life. Eat. Work. Sleep. Repeat. So where does anyone find time to pray? I admit, when I do find the time it feels like I'm just going through the motions. Like it's little more than an obligation." Sound familiar? Try pondering Revelation 3:20. In prayer we are not communing with a cold universe that cannot speak back or love us. With Jesus, prayer is speaking to a friend. And not just any friend. We are fellowshipping with the King of kings and Lord of lords—the One who created us in His image and cares about every detail of our lives.

There is a beautiful way of looking at prayer when we read Psalm 42:1 (ESV): "As a deer pants for flowing streams, so pants my soul for you, O God." Imagine a thirsty deer finally coming across a spring-fed stream. She dips her tongue into the cool swirling water and finds refreshment. The deer cannot survive without water, and so it is with us and the Lord. May we thirst for His life-giving fellowship!

*Jesus, I want to be in Your presence daily, not because of duty,
but because I love You and can't live without You! Amen.*

The Springs of Life

Keep your heart with all vigilance,
for from it flow the springs of life.
PROVERBS 4:23 ESV

Ages ago women used to chat over the back fence or over a cup of fresh coffee. They shared their hearts, their joys, their fears and sorrows. They felt refreshed from the encounter. They not only coped but they thrived in their communities.

But now in our obsessively fast-paced tech age, we're forced to deal with a much different society. There's a continuous onslaught of too much internet, too much cruel rhetoric on social media, too much evil glamorized on TV, too much frantic texting even while driving, and nonstop news with its up-close horrors from around the world.

We try to cope as best we can, but we have thousands of friends who aren't really friends and online communities that don't really offer the help and healing and personal touch of real community. We're superconnected, but we're not thriving as we should.

The Bible reminds us to keep watch over our hearts. There is good reason for that. The springs of life flow from our hearts. If we allow our spirits to become a dumping ground, the springs will get contaminated. They will become poisoned and unusable.

What to do? Unplug for a while. Spend more time with God and real friends. It will be a way to find our joy again.

Lord, show me when to unplug from this modern life. Amen.

Your Supernatural Care

Precious in the sight of the Lord
is the death of his faithful servants.
PSALM 116:15 NIV

Death has come to your loved one, and just when you thought you might be able to handle the shock, you realize you can't. Not at all. This is a goodbye that you can't accept. You officially fall into a million pieces right in front of the hospital staff. The relatives. And God. In between bouts of crying, you yelled at a nurse. You blamed the doctor. You feel alone, cold, and more frightened than you can ever remember. Telling yourself to be strong isn't going to be enough.

Know that God does care about His faithful servants when they are dying. This hospital scene is not taken lightly by the Lord. He considers this moment in time as you do—important and precious. His love is profound and His arms are sturdy. Let the Lord cool your feverish brow with His tender mercies. And allow the Lord's ministering angels—both the earthly kind and perhaps the heavenly kind—to bring you comfort.

Oh Almighty God, I come before You truly frightened.
I don't know how to carry this burden of loss. It is far
too heavy for me. I need Your supernatural care
right now. In Jesus' name I pray, amen.

Hope

In him we have redemption through his blood, the forgiveness of sins, in accordance with the riches of God's grace.

EPHESIANS 1:7 NIV

As you munch popcorn and watch a movie at your local cinema, you discover that one of the main characters is evil from the word go. He is angry at the world, he spews hate, and he seems utterly worthless to humanity. Then suddenly, you see a pause in his barrage of wickedness. Does he sense peace when he takes a step back from the darkness? Maybe. Then there's an epiphany as he witnesses the greater glory of a goodwill moment. Light shines on his face. There it is on the screen—what the audience has been waiting for.

Hope. Change. Life.

The question is, Were those moments fleeting or will that seed of change take root in the character's life? You watch the man's conversion unfold, and at the end, he is no longer the same person he was when he started his journey. He is transformed, and we leave the theater feeling joyful. Even if the Gospel message isn't fully presented, we love the very act of redemption.

God's redemption offered to us through Christ is the very best story, of course, but it's a story He hopes we won't just watch on the silver screen but really live forever!

Jesus, I thank You for Your redeeming love. It has made all the difference in my life—both now and for eternity! Amen.

We Need More Merry

A cheerful disposition is good for your health;
gloom and doom leave you bone-tired.
PROVERBS 17:22 MSG

Like a bungee cord stretched to the snapping limit, the tension in the meeting escalated until the whole group feared a meltdown or a mutiny. Everyone disagreed on everything, but no one was in the mood to compromise. Just as the committee chair was giving everyone the evil eye, one of the attenders decided to do something unexpected, guileless, and right-down silly. With tremendous seriousness, he slipped on a pair of wobbling reindeer antlers and began to take notes.

The oxygen left the room. No one really knew what to do or say. Then as if on some celestial cue, everybody burst out into thunderous laughter. Then someone got up and began pouring coffee and passing out the pastries.

Man, what a great feeling that day. What had built into a mean-spirited standoff was diffused by nothing more than a merry heart. The world could sure use more merry. Much, much more.

Lord, I want to be the person who brings a merry spirit into
the room. A woman who energizes people while making them
feel at ease. And then after lightening their hearts, perhaps
they will let me share the good news of the Gospel. Amen.

Blankie

"Can you fathom the mysteries of God? Can you probe the limits of the Almighty? They are higher than the heavens above—what can you do? They are deeper than the depths below—what can you know?"

Job 11:7–8 NIV

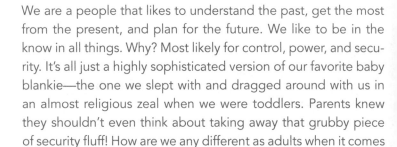

We are a people that likes to understand the past, get the most from the present, and plan for the future. We like to be in the know in all things. Why? Most likely for control, power, and security. It's all just a highly sophisticated version of our favorite baby blankie—the one we slept with and dragged around with us in an almost religious zeal when we were toddlers. Parents knew they shouldn't even think about taking away that grubby piece of security fluff! How are we any different as adults when it comes to larger life issues? When we get ahead of God or we waste our lives in worry, in many ways we still want some form of a blankie.

And yet who can know what tomorrow holds or fathom the mysteries of God, except to know that He is in control. But—mystery is a beautiful thing when it comes to faith in God. He is not only the almighty One; He is the just and loving One. He is the only One whom we can trust with our earthly lives and our eternal lives. And in that trust lies great joy!

*Lord, show me how to trust You with
my past, present, and future! Amen.*

She Really Gets My Goat!

"But I say to you, love your enemies, bless those who curse you, do good to those who hate you, and pray for those who spitefully use you and persecute you."
MATTHEW 5:44 NKJV

You can smell your new boss coming down the hallway. You used to love the smell of lavender perfume. But now? It makes you queasy. That woman has made your life miserable. She's never satisfied with your work. Never smiles. She is a walking booby trap. She makes a charging water buffalo look like an amateur at the art of trampling!

You might think, *I could be an outstanding Christian woman if I didn't have to deal with her. She always brings out the worst in me!*

What can you do? The Bible says to love your enemies. God also says to pray for her. You have no idea what kind of burdens she carries or how much she might be on the edge of a breakdown. When you do pray, you will help change her life, and the prayer will change your life as well. You will begin to see her through "God glasses."

Lord, I want to pray for _____. Please help and heal this person in every part of her life. And if she has never come to know You, please show her Your redeeming love. Amen.

Really Truly Forgiven?

The LORD is merciful and gracious, slow to anger and abounding in steadfast love. He will not always chide, nor will he keep his anger forever. He does not deal with us according to our sins, nor repay us according to our iniquities. For as high as the heavens are above the earth, so great is his steadfast love toward those who fear him; as far as the east is from the west, so far does he remove our transgressions from us.

PSALM 103:8–12 ESV

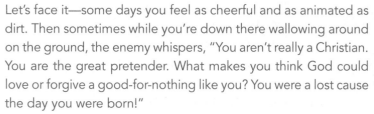

Let's face it—some days you feel as cheerful and as animated as dirt. Then sometimes while you're down there wallowing around on the ground, the enemy whispers, "You aren't really a Christian. You are the great pretender. What makes you think God could love or forgive a good-for-nothing like you? You were a lost cause the day you were born!"

You might agree and think, *Well, that's true. Sometimes I don't really feel forgiven.* But faith is not so much a feeling as a commitment to God and His promises of grace. Your sins are not so unique that God decided to bypass you when He offered salvation. If you repent and ask for forgiveness—then you have indeed been forgiven. It is that simple. It is that joyful!

Embrace the truth. Live the grace. Share the news!

Lord Jesus, thank You for washing my sins away. I choose to believe in Your promises! Amen.

Protection

Put on the whole armor of God, that you may be able to stand against the schemes of the devil. For we do not wrestle against flesh and blood, but against the rulers, against the authorities, against the cosmic powers over this present darkness, against the spiritual forces of evil in the heavenly places.

EPHESIANS 6:11–12 ESV

The woman threw on a light jacket for her stroll through the woods, but as she hiked along, the temperature plummeted and the snow flurries went from light to heavy. She panicked, knowing that her jacket wasn't providing nearly enough warmth, and the footpath was nearly covered in snow. Suddenly that joyful and invigorating walk through the woods had the potential to become deadly.

In this world, we are at the mercy of various dangerous spiritual elements that the Bible talks about. But as Christians, we are not without protection. Ephesians 6:14–17 (ESV) says it well: "Stand therefore, having fastened on the belt of truth, and having put on the breastplate of righteousness, and, as shoes for your feet, having put on the readiness given by the gospel of peace. In all circumstances take up the shield of faith, with which you can extinguish all the flaming darts of the evil one; and take the helmet of salvation, and the sword of the Spirit, which is the word of God."

Lord, thank You for giving me guidance and for showing me how to handle this veiled realm. Amen.

What I Want to Ask God

*Call to me and I will answer you, and will tell you
great and hidden things that you have not known.*
JEREMIAH 33:3 NRSV

Kids never stop asking questions. That is one of the ways they grow and learn. Somewhere in our journey to adulthood though, we stop asking so many questions, even of God. But if you could ask the Lord anything at all, what might you like to know?

How about these: Did You create humans because you felt a divine lonesomeness? Since the Bible speaks of perfumes and aromas, what is Your favorite scent? Were some living things created to be curious and amusing—such as the dumbo octopus, the wombat, the pink fairy armadillo, the peacock mantis shrimp, the blue dragon, the aye-aye, and the blob fish, to name a few? Is it possible to feel joy every day of an earthly life? If there is an end to the vast universe, what is beyond that?

There is a world of questions out there that sort of hang in the air between heaven and earth, and sometimes it is only God who has the answer to them. Never stop talking to God. He may not answer all of your questions until you are on the other side, but He loves to hear from His kids!

---

*Lord, I do have some questions that have
been on my mind. _____. Amen.*

Dust Yourself Off

And Jesus increased in wisdom and in
years, and in divine and human favor.
LUKE 2:52 NRSV

Okay, you've worked hard at maturing as a Christian woman, not because you're trying to manipulate your way into heaven, but because you're grateful to the Lord for all He's done. Then you decide to drive to your hometown, to stay in the house you grew up in, and to sleep in the bed of your youth. Oh dear. Pretty humbling, eh? There goes all that wisdom and maturity right out the window.

What is it about going back to one's childhood roots and remembering every stupid thing you ever did that can make you feel lost and juvenile and helpless? It can so emotionally wreck a woman that she's reduced to hiding in the corner making little spit bubbles.

It's the same when we stumble—yet again—on an old sin. Or out of the blue, we're riddled with terrible doubts in our faith. Or any number of moments that set us back in our faith walk.

Satan would like for you to give up. But don't take the bait. Let the Lord help you rise again, dust yourself off, and get back on the road to growing up into a woman of wisdom and joy!

Lord, I have failed. Forgive me.
Please set me back on the path of life! Amen.

It's the Little Things

"Give, and it will be given to you. Good measure, pressed down, shaken together, running over, will be put into your lap. For with the measure you use it will be measured back to you."
LUKE 6:38 ESV

There's a little jag in the country road, and in that nook is a tiny open hutch known to the locals as the Giving Box. Whenever anyone locally has some extra pears off their trees or more potatoes harvested than they can eat, they share them with their neighbors. This merry little enterprise is always done on the honor system, and it's always worked just fine. As the people in the community drive by, they don't always know why they find themselves smiling when they see the Giving Box, but they smile all the same. It could be because people like seeing that there is still some goodness in the world, still places where folks care about one another—for they do not give out of obligation but simply from their hearts. The Giving Box becomes a place of joy.

Yes, sometimes what is measured back to us from our giving is joy, and that joy is far greater than all the other treasures of this world.

I am thankful, Lord, for friends and family and a giving community. I know this pleases You when we have a generous heart. May I always relish the joy of giving! Amen.

He's Got You!

*Then they cried to the L*ORD *in their trouble,*
and he saved them from their distress.
PSALM 107:19 NIV

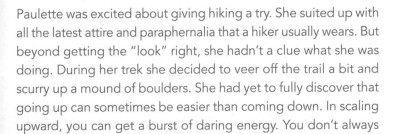

Paulette was excited about giving hiking a try. She suited up with all the latest attire and paraphernalia that a hiker usually wears. But beyond getting the "look" right, she hadn't a clue what she was doing. During her trek she decided to veer off the trail a bit and scurry up a mound of boulders. She had yet to fully discover that going up can sometimes be easier than coming down. In scaling upward, you can get a burst of daring energy. You don't always see the peril in the same way as when you're coming down. As it turned out, Paulette had indeed climbed too high for her beginner status. Up on top, her heartbeat boom-banged and her hands shimmied as she looked down at the various falling hazards all around her. Her mind screamed, "This is hopeless!"

Wisely, Paulette was hiking with a buddy who was more experienced. Step by step, this male friend helped her climb down toward safety. At one point in Paulette's panic, her friend grasped her hand and said with confidence, "I've got you."

Right then and probably for the rest of her life, Paulette would think those were some of the most beautiful words ever linked together. "I've got you!" Pure joy.

Lord, thank You that You've got me when
I'm in need of being rescued. Amen.

A Little Lighter on Their Feet

A gentle answer turns away wrath,
but a harsh word stirs up anger.
PROVERBS 15:1 NIV

Everybody in the break room could feel it coming. The two female coworkers—who were always at each other's throats—were about to blow again like twin volcanoes. The other employees all cowered and slunk around the room, trying to get a fresh cup of coffee without being dragged into the fiasco. Somebody whispered, "Why do they have to do this? Can't anyone give an inch?" But after woman number one dropped another little insult bomb, the other gal paused.

Everyone in the break room cringed, waiting for the inevitable explosion from the bucket of gasoline that woman number two would surely toss onto the verbal blaze. But then the most unexpected thing happened. The second gal didn't reply with anger as usual. She calmed herself and said, "It's okay. You know what? I think that's an interesting point. Thanks."

Woman number one was so taken off guard with the sudden friendly concession—the gentle answer—she stumbled all over her words and sputtered out in a whimper. Her wrath had run out of fuel, so the fire died. Everyone in the break room sighed with relief, sipped their coffee, and then went back to work a little lighter on their feet.

Lord, may I always take time to pause and breathe
a prayer before I let go with a verbal barb. Amen.

Instant Joy

*Therefore encourage one another and build
each other up, just as in fact you are doing.*
1 THESSALONIANS 5:11 NIV

We love instant everything, don't we? High-speed communication. News in sound bites. Fast food. Faster cars. But what about instant joy?

If you think about women in your church, friends, coworkers, your child's teachers, and family, you can probably name quite a few folks who are discouraged in one way or the other. Maybe they seem to be running on fumes, worn out from all kinds of earthly trials. It costs us nothing but a bit of time to give the gift that people desperately need. That is, a kind and heartfelt word of encouragement. It might be that a friend needs to know she is doing a good job volunteering at church, and that her time and talent are truly appreciated. It might be that you've forgotten to remind your father how much he means to you. Perhaps there's a widow down the street who needs a smile and a sincere compliment. Maybe you could send a note to your child's teacher, praising her for something she did well. Who are all the people you can bring instant joy to today?

*Holy Spirit, please tell me who might need a
special word of encouragement. I am willing
and able to spread some joy! Amen.*

The Wedding at Cana

When the master of the feast tasted the water now become wine, and did not know where it came from (though the servants who had drawn the water knew), the master of the feast called the bridegroom and said to him, "Everyone serves the good wine first, and when people have drunk freely, then the poor wine. But you have kept the good wine until now." This, the first of his signs, Jesus did at Cana in Galilee, and manifested his glory. And his disciples believed in him.
JOHN 2:9–11 ESV

There is much to glean from this wedding story. First, Jesus made it obvious that He respected His mother by honoring her wishes. Also, the Lord must have felt compassion for the families involved, not wanting them to be embarrassed by running out of beverages at the wedding. But that isn't all—Jesus didn't bother transforming the water into ordinary wine. He made the best, and the best was fully noticed and deeply appreciated!

Jesus prepared the best for this couple in Cana, and He helped to make it a special and memorable wedding for everyone invited. Yes, Jesus is about redemption and eternal life, but He is also about providing what is best for us, including joy!

Lord, I thank You that You offer humankind the best of everything, including the gift of joy. Amen.

With Gentleness Comes Joy

To slander no one, to be peaceable and considerate,
and always to be gentle toward everyone.
TITUS 3:2 NIV

Oh, for the gentle things in life. We need more and more since the opposite has driven away our joy. What are your favorite "gentle gifts"? The soft coos of your baby just before she drifts off to sleep. The afternoon sun as it sprays a mellow glow over your garden. Your child's hand snuggly holding yours. A stream burbling its way down the hillside. The tranquility of a few hours swaying in your hammock. Your beloved brushing your hair and whispering, "I love you." And of course, the best gentle gift is an attitude of goodwill toward humankind—even when it's not Christmas.

In Galatians 5:22–23 (NIV) we are reminded, "But the fruit of the Spirit is love, joy, peace, forbearance, kindness, goodness, faithfulness, gentleness and self-control. Against such things there is no law."

Somewhere deep down we all long for more of the gentle things in life. With gentleness come the springs of joy.

God, I pray that You will give me tenderness of heart.
That I will never slander anyone, and that I will be
peaceful and considerate and gentle in all
my ways. In Jesus' name I pray, amen.

You Lack Nothing

*Consider it a sheer gift, friends, when tests and challenges
come at you from all sides. You know that under pressure,
your faith-life is forced into the open and shows its true
colors. So don't try to get out of anything prematurely.
Let it do its work so you become mature and
well-developed, not deficient in any way.*

JAMES 1:2–4 MSG

If you see danger coming, you naturally want to flee the scene.
In all honesty, we tend to run away from anything that takes
too much time, that is inconvenient, or that might cause us any
kind of pain. In other words, we want a good life, a risk-free life.
Basically, an easy life.

But even Jesus tells us that there will be trials. It is a fallen
earth, not heaven. When troubles do come, you don't have to
throw a party, but see what the Lord might do to use this hard
situation in your life. He knows the long-term plan while we only
see tiny pieces of a puzzle. He knows how beautiful the outcome
can be. He is hoping that you will grow into a woman who is so
full of faith and goodness and love and joy that you lack nothing.

---

*Lord, I admit I rarely see hardships as a gift. Show me
how to see this life from Your vantage point. I want
You to use my trials for spiritual growth. Amen.*

Not to Be Missed!

But nothing unclean will enter it, nor anyone who
practices abomination or falsehood, but only those
who are written in the Lamb's book of life.
REVELATION 21:27 NRSV

Your friend just got back from touring northern Italy by car. She raved about the majestic peaks of the Alps, the fragrant foothills, and the crystal lakes. Then there were the ancient castles and fairy-tale hamlets covered in ethereal mist. "Pure poetry," she said. At last she seemed overwhelmed from speaking of it and sighed. "What else can I say? It's simply *not* to be missed!"

And so it is with heaven. Jesus says He is preparing a place for us, His followers. And we should not only believe Him but look forward to that homegoing with anticipation and joy.

But do remember, if you want the glories of heaven, you can't just choose heaven—you must choose the way, the truth, and the life—Jesus Christ. Just in case you've never heard the good news, in John 3:16 (ESV) it says, "For God so loved the world, that he gave his only Son, that whoever believes in him should not perish but have eternal life."

Yes, heaven will be wonderful beyond our imaginings. It is simply not to be missed!

Lord, forgive me for my sins. I truly repent. I accept
You as my Savior. Please be the Lord of my life
both now and forevermore. Amen.

The Best Place to Be

You make known to me the path of life;
in your presence there is fullness of joy;
at your right hand are pleasures forevermore.
PSALM 16:11 ESV

People love sweet tea. So satisfying and, well, sweet! If you could bottle joy like sweet tea, that product would be the top-selling beverage of all time. Why? Because people are sick and tired of being unhappy. They are worn ragged trying to gather up what they think might bring them a few moments of happiness. They search and buy and beg and hope, but at the end of the day their own futile attempts at joy produce nothing that will truly fill their souls. The problem is they are trying to fix a spiritual need with a worldly bandage. It simply won't work.

What *does* work is to bask in the presence of God. But the Lord wants more from us than just to show up in a room waiting for our allotment of joy. He wants us to have a longing to truly spend time with Him, not out of obligation or with a mind-set to manipulate some gift out of Him, but because we truly have a need to be with Christ because we love Him dearly.

With that attitude in mind, come rest in the Lord. In His sweet and satisfying presence, you will find fullness of joy and pleasures forevermore. It's the best place to be!

Lord, I am excited to be with You today. Amen.

Fooling Ourselves

*But prove yourselves doers of the word [actively and
continually obeying God's precepts], and not merely listeners
[who hear the word but fail to internalize its meaning], deluding
yourselves [by unsound reasoning contrary to the truth].*
JAMES 1:22 AMP

Humans love the truth, or so they say. Sometimes, they will
shake their fists and shout all over the place demanding it from
everyone—but themselves. One instance that reveals our double
standard concerns God's command that we live in obedience to
His Word.

Think of it this way: living outside of the Lord's guidelines is a
real joy killer. Wild living won't be a friend to us in the end. What
might feel like pleasure for a time will morph into pain. Why would
we really want to do anything that could destroy us in body and
soul? It's hard to expect showers of blessings from the Lord when
we are rebelliously bathing in sin.

So step boldly out into the light of God's Word. Live the truth.
Taste the freedom. God will only ask us to do what will ultimately
bring us what we really want—love and peace and real joy!

*Lord, I have been fooling myself, living a lifestyle that is in
opposition to Your precepts. Forgive me, and give me the
courage to do what is right and good in Your sight. Amen.*

When Joy Feels Far Away

You turned my wailing into dancing; you removed my sackcloth and clothed me with joy, that my heart may sing your praises and not be silent. LORD my God, I will praise you forever.
PSALM 30:11–12 NIV

It really is okay to weep. We have been given tear ducts by our Creator, so He must have thought we'd need them. Even Jesus wept and was referred to as a man of sorrows. We are in good company when we mourn. Ecclesiastes reminds us that there is a time for weeping and laughing, for mourning and dancing. This broken planet is not an easy place to live, and sometimes joy seems like no more than a dream.

Whether you're grieving the loss of someone dear or you're wounded deeply over a different kind of tragedy, give yourself some time to grieve, to pray, to recover. Be gentle with yourself. Rest. And then remind God of His promises that He will turn your lamenting into laughter. That He will clothe you once again in joy.

Dearest Lord Jesus, I am grieving. I see now that I cannot recover from my loss without Your supernatural help. May Your Comforter, the Holy Spirit, bring me relief for my aching soul. And may I someday wake up to Your joy again. Amen.

Dump the Worry Glasses

Anxiety weighs down the heart,
but a kind word cheers it up.
PROVERBS 12:25 NIV

The woman slipped on her dark worry glasses. They fit pretty well, but after a while, they did grind into the flesh and leave some pretty ugly red marks on her nose. But well, she was used to them, so she put up with the annoyance and pain. The other problem was that the lenses were so dark that she couldn't see life clearly. When she did wear them, she noticed a plethora of possible perils to worry about. You know, she agonized about the loneliness she might experience when empty nest arrived. She stewed about why her friend didn't give her a thumbs-up on social media. She got anxious about what her neighbors thought of her plastic pink flamingoes on the front lawn. She would wring her hands over her diet, her marriage, her talent or lack of it, her latest facial wrinkle. When she had on her worry glasses, everything had fretting potential!

But what she couldn't see while wearing those dark glasses was the joy. It was all around her like colorful confetti, and yet every day she missed it.

Lord, I confess that I slip on those worry glasses
way too often. Help me to trust You with all
of my life, so I don't miss the joy! Amen.

Custom Built

*Oh yes, you shaped me first inside, then out; you formed
me in my mother's womb. I thank you, High God—you're
breathtaking! Body and soul, I am marvelously made!
I worship in adoration—what a creation! You know me
inside and out, you know every bone in my body; You
know exactly how I was made, bit by bit, how I was
sculpted from nothing into something. Like an open book,
you watched me grow from conception to birth; all the
stages of my life were spread out before you, the days
of my life all prepared before I'd even lived one day.*
PSALM 139:13–16 MSG

Haute couture is high fashion. It is exclusive, unique, and known for its extraordinary quality. It is made by gifted creators and sewn with attention to every detail. Wow, sounds pretty wonderful, right?

Sometimes we humans get into the mind-set that we are cookie-cutter common. This discouraging notion that we are nothing unique or special may come from online articles, TV, social media, strangers, or even family and friends! Well, don't you believe it! That isn't what the Bible says. You are marvelously custom created and hand sewn by God Himself. Not mass-produced or churned out. You, my friend, are human haute couture!

*I thank You, Lord, that I am fearfully
and marvelously made by You! Amen.*

Getting Ahead of God

Now Sarai, Abram's wife, had borne him no children. But she had an Egyptian slave named Hagar; so she said to Abram, "The LORD has kept me from having children. Go, sleep with my slave; perhaps I can build a family through her." Abram agreed to what Sarai said.
GENESIS 16:1–2 NIV

Exasperated, Linda blew the bangs off her forehead for the last time. She marched into the bathroom, took a pair of shears, and gave her bangs a vigorous trim. Oh no. She now had this frizzy-haired, cockatoo thing going on at the top of her head. Oy! Not the look she was going for. She berated herself for her impulsiveness. But the sudden action didn't surprise her, since it had been a lifelong problem—getting ahead of common sense.

And a bigger problem in her life was that she often got ahead of God too. She could relate to Sarah in the Bible who had a similar problem. Since God wasn't working on Sarah's timetable, she decided to produce a child in a way that brought hardship to her and her family. Linda sighed, wondering how she could curb this flaw in her personality. Perhaps for starters, she could pray for patience, trust God more, and remember how in the past God did come through for her. Right. On. Time.

Yes, within a simple act called trust comes the beautiful blessing of joy!

Lord, please show me how to trust
You more completely. Amen.

Getting Off the Treadmill

*I am not saying this because I am in need, for I have learned
to be content whatever the circumstances. I know what it
is to be in need, and I know what it is to have plenty. I have
learned the secret of being content in any and every situation,
whether well fed or hungry, whether living in plenty or in
want. I can do all this through him who gives me strength.*
PHILIPPIANS 4:11–13 NIV

Suzanna met a wild-eyed stranger in the department store checkout line who'd obviously had too much caffeine. The woman could *not* stop talking. She said, "You know, my husband and I built a new house. It's got everything. A spa, outdoor kitchen, swimming pool, and tennis court. I personally discovered that less is definitely not more. Don't you think? Of course, you understand. Anyway, my husband and I take our responsibilities as consumers seriously. We feel it's our patriotic duty to buy more to boost our economy. So, I'm here today buying and boosting." The woman giggled riotously.

Suzanna's eye twitched. She suddenly had a desire to go home and purge a few belongings.

It is dangerously easy to get on the materialistic treadmill and not be able to get off until you're forced to. Sometimes "more" really isn't better—it is just more, and it has the potential to bring you more anxiety than joy.

Lord, show me how to be content with what I have. Amen.

The Way We Love God

"Teacher, which is the greatest commandment in the Law?"
Jesus replied: "'Love the Lord your God with all your
heart and with all your soul and with all your mind.'"
MATTHEW 22:36–37 NIV

You may love your home and enjoy your career and hobbies, but as you ponder various kinds of affections for things, you realize that none of it would mean anything if something happened to your family. Because you know in your heart what is precious. You know what you need to be happy—what you can't live without.

Is that the same way we love God? Or do we love Him even more? Over the years have we discovered that we simply can't live without His company day or night? In good times or bad? That the Lord's mercy and grace, His divine guidance and perfect love can't come from any other source?

If you find yourself saying yes to the above, then you are not being vulnerable or weak or needy. You are being wise, for loving God with all your heart, soul, and mind is the way to grow into a woman of joy!

Lord Jesus, I love You dearly. I thank You for who You are and all You've done for me. May we stay forever close. Amen.

Toss the Sludge

Fools show their anger at once,
but the prudent ignore an insult.
PROVERBS 12:16 NRSV

You had the best lunch ever with your old friend, but on the drive home, some of her words kept playing in your head. Her comments could have been a mistake or a lighthearted jab or something much worse—a pointed insult. Should you call her up when you get home and give her a verbal poke to see what she really meant? Or should you be wise and let it go, giving her the benefit of the doubt?

It's like someone is offering you two different glasses of water to drink. One is fresh and cool and clean, and the second glass has some weird gunk floating in it—stuff that looks like it has the potential to make you miserable and sick. You would, of course, choose the pure one, right? It's the one that is meant for you to drink. And so it goes with our thoughts about people.

Accept the life-giving water. Toss the sludge.

Dear God, I admit I spend way too much time picking apart conversations, thinking the worst of people and their intentions. Even if someone means to insult me, please give me the prudence and courage to ignore their comments. In Jesus' name I pray, amen.

Who Has the Joy?

*Do not withhold good from those to whom
it is due, when it is in your power to act.*

The line at the pharmacy counter is a whopper. You have a brutal case of gout, and you think you might die of pain while you're waiting on your meds. So you mention the situation to the two gals in the line in front of you. One lady smiles and offers you her space immediately. The next gal gives in, but she does it hesitantly and with a bit of an evil eye. This second response has made you feel even worse if that were possible.

It's obvious which woman will have the greater joy as she drifts off to sleep. Most likely it'll be the woman who readily offered her spot, rather than the woman who did so begrudgingly.

Yes, it's true that there's always a chance someone is taking advantage of us in a situation like the one presented, but wouldn't Christ want us to err on the side of compassion? After all, God has shown us all great mercy. It would be one more way for us to thank Him.

Oh Lord, in the past, sometimes I have been stingy when it comes to good deeds, especially if I'm in a hurry. Please give me patience and a big heart for people. Amen.

Breezy

Do not be anxious about anything,
but in every situation, by prayer and petition,
with thanksgiving, present your requests to God.
PHILIPPIANS 4:6 NIV

The poor woman hadn't slept in days. She had been overwrought with a heavy burden for her grandson. The young man was in the middle of a rebellious season, and everyone in the family had become exhausted talking to him, praying about him, and worrying over him.

Sleepless and miserable, the grandmother finally got up in the middle of the night, got on her knees, and begged God for mercy. And then mercy arrived, but not as she expected. Relief came in the form of one word.

Breezy.

But why that word? What could the Lord mean? she wondered. But before her questions were finished, she knew deep down what it meant. She had always loved that word. It made her shoulders relax and her mouth curl up in a smile as she headed back to bed. To her, the word meant lighthearted with a touch of wind in one's hair. It even meant jolly. Basically, God expected her to rest easy while He worked on the problem. As humans, we can only do so much. At some point we have to trust the Lord with everything. Our lives. Our careers. Our health. Our loved ones. Everything.

What does God want you to become *breezy* about today?

Lord, help me to trust You with all the people I love,
knowing You love them even more than I do. Amen.

When You're Angry

*"In your anger do not sin": Do not let the
sun go down while you are still angry.*
EPHESIANS 4:26 NIV

Anger is as common as rain, and yet if we keep stewing in it, the
anger will turn into bitterness and sin. It will also make us sour
and sick. Not to mention how it will rob our joy and waste our
valuable time! As humans we have a need to organize and put
things in their proper place. Well, there is most certainly a good
and proper place for all that anger at the end of the day: at the
foot of the cross of Jesus. He is the only One who knows what
to do when our emotions run out of control. Give Christ the misunderstandings. The old baggage. The new baggage. The verbal
attacks and reckless words that linger with their wounds. All of it.
Place it there at His feet. And then walk away.

When you leave it there, don't revisit it. Don't drag it back.
Move forward with life.

Yes, anger is easy. Forgiveness is hard. But Christ can make
our burdens light. Let Him help. He's the only One who can.

*Too many times, Lord, I've gone to bed angry at someone.
Help me to reject the anger and embrace Your joy. Amen.*

Don't Pounce—Pray

As a prisoner for the Lord, then, I urge you to live a life worthy of the calling you have received. Be completely humble and gentle; be patient, bearing with one another in love.
EPHESIANS 4:1–2 NIV

Do you have a friend that you have to walk on eggshells around? That anything you say or do can be used against you? That she doesn't seem willing to give you the benefit of the doubt? She might even appear to relish your spiritual blunders so she can pelt you with her wise counsel! Wow, now there's a recipe that won't cook up any joy, eh? There's no happiness for the person who's continually walking on eggshells or for the person who is acting hypersensitive and sanctimonious.

But all of us are guilty of being too touchy and self-righteous at times. All of us need more forbearance and humility, gentleness and patience. How can we acquire these virtues? First recognize that all of humanity is in great need of these godly qualities—not just the other person. Then we need to ask the Holy Spirit to help us mature in this particular area of our lives.

May we all learn to pray rather than pounce!

Dearest Lord, forgive me that I am sometimes pompous and too quick to take offense. I need more forbearance, humility, gentleness, and patience. Amen.

Something's Going On

For our struggle is not against flesh and blood,
but against the rulers, against the authorities,
against the powers of this dark world and against
the spiritual forces of evil in the heavenly realms.

EPHESIANS 6:12 NIV

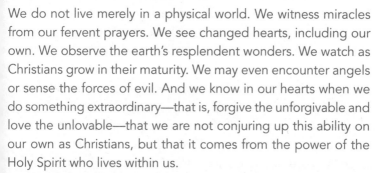

We do not live merely in a physical world. We witness miracles from our fervent prayers. We see changed hearts, including our own. We observe the earth's resplendent wonders. We watch as Christians grow in their maturity. We may even encounter angels or sense the forces of evil. And we know in our hearts when we do something extraordinary—that is, forgive the unforgivable and love the unlovable—that we are not conjuring up this ability on our own as Christians, but that it comes from the power of the Holy Spirit who lives within us.

If you sometimes feel like a skeptic, ask God to open your spiritual eyes even more—to be able to sense more clearly the supernatural realm. The Lord may surprise you.

Yes, the unseen world. It's there. It's real. And it's one more reason to follow Christ closely, because otherwise we are left to battle this dark world on our own. And that's not a war we can win without Christ.

Lord, be ever near me as I struggle against the rulers, against the authorities, against the powers of this dark world, and against the spiritual forces of evil in the heavenly realms. Amen.

The Joy of Being Rescued

"Suppose one of you has a hundred sheep and loses one of them. Doesn't he leave the ninety-nine in the open country and go after the lost sheep until he finds it?"
LUKE 15:4 NIV

Being lost, especially in the dark, can be frightening and deadly. Because in that darkness we stumble around. We don't know what's out there, what can harm us, or what can trip us up and cause us to fall into an abyss. In that lost state we can't even think straight—what we want for lunch, our favorite hobbies, or our work. All we can think about is being rescued, because that is obviously the top priority.

In this world, in our fallen state, sometimes that desperate need to be saved gets blurred or drowned out. Our obvious spiritual need is made not so obvious. Why? Because of our busyness. Because of the false narrative of friends or what the latest social media guru is promoting. Or because of the lies of Satan.

Want joy? There is no greater joy than when Jesus comes to rescue you. That glorious moment of a divine embrace. So acknowledge the need. Reach out to the Lord. He's calling your name, and He wants to bring you home, to love you for all time.

---

*Dearest Lord Jesus, thank You for
the joy of being rescued! Amen.*

The Perfect Gift

For it is by grace you have been saved, through faith—
and this is not from yourselves, it is the gift of God—
not by works, so that no one can boast.
EPHESIANS 2:8–9 NIV

From a delicious meal to the most beautiful garden we can think to create, it seems we can always come up with more improvements. We like to tweak and polish and add to things until we feel we've come as close to perfection as we can. But one thing that does not need tweaking of any kind, one thing that is complete in every way, is salvation through Christ. His sacrifice on the cross did it all. There are no works—whatsoever—that will get us into heaven. We only need to accept Jesus' perfect work of grace.

So beware of any religion that claims you need to add something to what Jesus has already provided. That would clearly be a religion of man, not a relationship with Christ.

Yes, we will naturally want to offer God some lovely gifts of service simply out of gratitude for His grace, but nothing we do will get us into heaven. Nothing. What a relief! What a magnificent and completely sufficient work of grace. We can rest in that. Praise our Lord Jesus, who has done it all for us. Out of mercy. Out of love. For me. For you. . .

Thank You, Lord, for Your sacrifice on the cross.
It means everything to me! Amen.

A Change of Focus

For by the grace given me I say to every one of you:
Do not think of yourself more highly than you ought,
but rather think of yourself with sober judgment, in
accordance with the faith God has distributed to each of you.
ROMANS 12:3 NIV

Have you ever known someone who lived her life with an egotistical attitude of "It's all about me"? Of course, there's no chance that the person is you! But there are times when we all romance a "me, me" mentality. Two questions—among many—that we could ask ourselves are "Do I often monopolize the conversation and manipulate discussions so that people are forced to deal with *my* needs, *my* views, and *my* accomplishments?" Or, "Am I only pretending to listen to others, while I'm really cooking up what *I'll* say next?"

Do we assume we have arrived on the scene of life and everyone is just lucky to be in our presence? Or do we have a sober judgment of ourselves and enter into conversations thinking of the needs of others first? May the Lord help us find a joyful balance between knowing that we are children of the King and knowing that we are to have the heart of a servant.

Lord, teach me Your ways, that I might
focus on others rather than myself. Amen.

We Are Not Our Own

Do you not know that your body is a temple of the Holy Spirit who is within you, whom you have [received as a gift] from God, and that you are not your own [property]? You were bought with a price [you were actually purchased with the precious blood of Jesus and made His own]. So then, honor and glorify God with your body.
1 CORINTHIANS 6:19–20 AMP

Sometimes we overdo it on those gooey doughnuts covered in confection. Right? Or we gorge on those whopper-sized, bacon-wrapped burgers entombed in cheese. Or we find ourselves in a cud-chewing frenzy with a bowl of no-name candy that looks more like little plastic toys than real food!

And while we use our bodies like garbage disposals, could we also be guilty of indulging in junk food for the soul? We might pour television shows, movies, internet sites, books, and social media down the hatch without much discretion or discernment on how it affects our spirits.

But our bodies, minds, and spirits are not like a landfill site. We are bought with a price with the precious blood of Christ. We are not our own. As Christians, may we never grieve the Holy Spirit—who lives within us—but instead, may we honor God in every way, including with our bodies.

Holy Spirit, please give me the discipline to do what is right with my body, and may my obedience bring us both joy! Amen.

Oh, How She Sparkled!

"You are the light of the world. A town built on a hill cannot be hidden. Neither do people light a lamp and put it under a bowl. Instead they put it on its stand, and it gives light to everyone in the house. In the same way, let your light shine before others, that they may see your good deeds and glorify your Father in heaven."
MATTHEW 5:14–16 NIV

Gracie breezed into the holiday party like a lit Christmas tree. Oh, how she sparkled. Her hair glowed, her shimmer-powder glistened, and her sequined dress looked positively electric! As she whirled and flitted and laughed, people took notice. They smiled. They nodded. It is fun to sparkle at a party.

As Christians, hopefully people will notice more than our party sparkle. May people also notice that the illumination we give off is not just from pretty powders but from the light of Christ who shines within us. For this kind of sublime glow cannot be washed off in the shower at the end of the day, because it is a holy glow that is divine and blessed and eternal!

---

*Mighty God, please let my light shine
so that I might be a powerful witness to
Your truth! In Jesus' name I pray, amen.*

A Good and Godly Habit

*Cast your cares on the L*ORD *and he will sustain you;*
he will never let the righteous be shaken.
PSALM 55:22 NIV

You start the day feeling pretty light, but before you know it, you start picking up little worry marbles along the way. The homework that your kids didn't get done. The cough your husband can't seem to get rid of. The church's sudden decision to fire a beloved pastor. A friend who refuses to call you back. The loss of a beloved pet. The presentation at work that was less than stellar. Before you know it, your empty bag is weighted down with heavy worry marbles. You find yourself dragging around that bag until you look up and remember that you are to cast those cares on the Lord.

And you do. Then once again, you see that it makes a big difference in your life—that is, between misery and joy.

In fact, if you write out your woes in a journal, you may go back to discover with some amazement that the things you worried about have now become no more than a hazy memory.

Lord, I confess that I too often find myself fretting, which
means I am not trusting You as I should. May I learn the
good and godly habit of casting my cares on You. Amen.

Unanswered Prayer

*And he withdrew from them about a stone's throw,
and knelt down and prayed, saying, "Father, if you are
willing, remove this cup from me. Nevertheless, not
my will, but yours, be done." And there appeared
to him an angel from heaven, strengthening him.*
LUKE 22:41–43 ESV

What are we to do with, what seems to us, an unanswered prayer? We might think, *If God doesn't give me what I want, then He must not care about me, or He must not love me. Or maybe I don't possess enough faith.*

And yet Jesus' own passionate prayer in the garden of Gethsemane—which caused Him to sweat great drops of blood—was not answered in the way He had hoped. Jesus knew He was loved by His Father. Jesus knew He had the necessary faith, and yet God did not remove His cup of sorrow.

But Jesus also prayed, "Not my will, but yours, be done." Jesus didn't receive what He'd first prayed for that night, but His heavenly appeal also showed us that He was willing to give Himself up for us. In Christ's loving surrender, His death and resurrection then became the greatest miracle of all time. So, if our prayers get answered in a different way, could it be there is a divine and eternal purpose that we can't quite see yet? May we also pray, "Not my will, but Yours, be done."

Lord, in all my prayers, Your will be done. Amen.

Reasons for Our Joy!

*"In my Father's house there are many dwelling places.
If it were not so, would I have told you that I
go to prepare a place for you?"*
JOHN 14:2 NRSV

As Christians, we have reason to sing, to rejoice, to laugh and dance and shout for joy. We have the beauty of forgiveness, the assurance of salvation, and the anticipation of heaven. May that amazing truth trickle deep down into our spirits so it can become part of our everyday lives. So that when the time is right, we can be a sunburst of good news in a world of storms.

When we do share our faith, we don't need to lecture, but we should explain the reasons for our joy. After all, we don't represent a religion riddled and burdened with endless works and impossible strivings, but we represent the powerful promise of life eternal in Christ.

Hold fast to the truth. Let our faces reflect that hope. And may we show the world what joy really looks like!

Dear Jesus, too many times I get so wrapped up in the world's way of seeing life and death, I forget that there is much more beyond the confines of this broken earth. I praise You and thank You for the hope of heaven! Amen.

Embrace the Quiet

She had a sister called Mary, who sat at the Lord's feet listening to what he said. But Martha was distracted by all the preparations that had to be made. She came to him and asked, "Lord, don't you care that my sister has left me to do the work by myself? Tell her to help me!" "Martha, Martha," the Lord answered, "you are worried and upset about many things, but few things are needed—or indeed only one. Mary has chosen what is better, and it will not be taken away from her."
LUKE 10:39–42 NIV

If you have the gift of hospitality, then people love coming to your house because you are welcoming and organized, and you probably put on one gorgeous buffet! But there is a time for being a good hostess, and there is a time to sit quietly at Jesus' feet.

Satan wants our days to be so hectic, loud, and distorted that we find few minutes for these quiet times. You know, those moments when you might find yourself growing in God's wisdom, confidence, and joy. You might discover the Lord's guidance, tender rebukes, and sweet encouragements. You might commune so closely that you feel His presence in the room with you. Don't run from the quiet. Embrace it. And be aware that you might be changed by the risen Savior!

Lord, may I wait in Your presence
with anticipation and joy! Amen.

A Force of Nature

*And do not be conformed to this world [any longer
with its superficial values and customs], but be transformed
and progressively changed [as you mature spiritually] by
the renewing of your mind [focusing on godly values and
ethical attitudes], so that you may prove [for yourselves]
what the will of God is, that which is good and acceptable
and perfect [in His plan and purpose for you].*
ROMANS 12:2 AMP

Needing to be part of a club is a powerful force of nature. We feel that tug through school when we want to have all the same toys as our friends and we want to dress the same quirky way and eat the same weird foods. We crave that connection, that fellowship. That "belonging."

Then as adults we act the same way—just on a more sophisticated level—wanting to be connected to a tribe, but that crowd might not always be spiritually healthy. It might make us feel accepted and maybe even loved, but it may also infuse us with so much of the world's values, customs, ethics, and lifestyles that we find ourselves straying far from Christ and His precepts.

If you want to be transformed in Christ and not conformed to the world, don't forget to fellowship with the body of believers and spend time in God's Word. The Lord wants to show you what is good and acceptable and perfect!

Lord, help me to be a spiritually mature woman of God. Amen.

What Will You Leave Behind?

*But the fruit of the Spirit [the result of His presence
within us] is love [unselfish concern for others], joy,
[inner] peace, patience [not the ability to wait, but how
we act while waiting], kindness, goodness, faithfulness.*
GALATIANS 5:22 AMP

We will all leave things behind when we pass from this earth. Yes, all our material goods will, of course, be either passed down, given away, sold, or tossed. But we will also leave lots of other "effects" behind. Things that are much more important and lasting than mere possessions.

On that day when people gather around your body, what will they say about you? Were people's lives made better because you were born? Did you mature in Christ, and did your life display the various sweet and nourishing fruits of the Spirit? Did people come to know Christ because of your witness of the Gospel? If you had children, did they rise up and call you blessed because of your faithful living testimony? Did you sprinkle joy and truth and love wherever you went? These are our choices—daily. What kind of legacy will you leave behind?

*Lord, I want to possess all the fruits of the Spirit.
I don't want to just talk about them and teach them;
I want to live them fully for Your glory. Amen.*

Behind the Scenes

And we know [with great confidence] that God [who is deeply concerned about us] causes all things to work together [as a plan] for good for those who love God, to those who are called according to His plan and purpose.
ROMANS 8:28 AMP

Right from the very beginning, good parents are working to make their child's life healthy and happy. Good parents want the best for their children mentally, physically, and spiritually. They are ever working behind the scenes to make family life better. They spend long hours feeding, diapering, rocking, dreaming, doctoring, coddling, and loving. And that's just in the first week!

God is also working behind the scenes on our behalf, doing what a good parent would do. While we do love our kids, we are not perfect, so no matter how hard we might try, we're going to occasionally drop the ball. But the Lord is perfect in His parenting, and we can know with confidence that the Lord not only cares deeply for us, but He is actively working on our behalf, reshaping our mess into something magnificent.

Almighty God, thank You for being the perfect loving parent, and thank You for taking my hardships and errors and turning them into something good. I trust You and I love You dearly! In Jesus' name I pray, amen.

Give Me Patience!

"But I tell you, love your enemies and
pray for those who persecute you."
MATTHEW 5:44 NIV

Okay, you've moved forward in your maturity in Christ. Good!
Even your friends and family have noticed. You feel heart-close
to the Lord, and you've even been blessed with a love for all
humanity. Excellent!

And then your Aunt Zelma shows up for a visit.

All bets are off. Yeah, any ground you gained may be lost in
one hour of her company. And joy will only be a memory. Aunt
Zelma knows just which buttons to push with her pointy little
finger. You now jerk into high alert, waiting for her to judge you,
insult you, control you, laugh at you, not to mention push away
your pound cake, saying it is too bland for her taste!

What is a body to do? Pray for your enemies. Pray for
patience. Pray you can find joy and give joy even when you're
surrounded by controlling and testy people. Take comfort in the
fact that everyone has an Aunt Zelma—someone who seems to
be strategically placed in our lives so that we can learn to grow
in patience and forgiveness.

And know too that you might be an Aunt Zelma to someone
else—and she might have to pray for patience when she sees
you coming.

Lord, please give me patience the way
You have patience with me. Amen.

That Beautiful Bridge

*That God is on one side and all the people on
the other side, and Christ Jesus, himself man,
is between them to bring them together.*
1 TIMOTHY 2:5 TLB

The two gal friends loved having coffee and fellowship together every morning, but they didn't love the muddy ditch they had to cross to get to each other's house. So, an older neighbor friend who was retired decided to build a little wooden bridge over that mucky gully to make their lives better. He worked hard on the structure, using only the best materials. In the end, it was a fine piece of workmanship—strong and usable and even beautiful. The two women were astounded and deeply appreciative. They wanted to pay him for his work, but the man refused any sort of compensation. And yet, he did agree to come over for coffee.

Christ is that dear friend who built us a bridge to God, to heaven. He made that bridge because He loves us, and He built that bridge with His very life. We can never repay the Lord for what He did on the cross, but we can thank Him by inviting Him in for coffee and fellowship. He will be there!

*Dearest Lord Jesus, thank You for being the
bridge that paved my way to heaven. Amen.*

Rejoice in the Lord!

*Though the fig tree should not blossom, nor fruit
be on the vines, the produce of the olive fail and the
fields yield no food, the flock be cut off from the fold
and there be no herd in the stalls, yet I will rejoice in
the LORD; I will take joy in the God of my salvation.*
<small>HABAKKUK 3:17–18 ESV</small>

Here's a mind game people like to play. "I will know joy when I finally recover from this terrible physical ailment. I need good health for joy. Well, and I could also use a perfect spouse, perfect kids, a perfect career, and a perfect church just to name a few extra things."

The problem with that mind game is that when we play it, we will never win. We will never experience joy or have a reason to rejoice. We will just be a soul in a constant state of neediness. And humans are needy. No doubt about it. But God says to find joy even when we're in the midst of trials and trouble.

In this life, there will always be problems and difficulties to deal with. Always. So, trust now. Rejoice in the Lord today. Live now!

---

*Lord, I rejoice in this new day. Together You
and I will make the most of it! Amen.*

Spiritually Vulnerable

*All Scripture is breathed out by God and profitable for
teaching, for reproof, for correction, and for training
in righteousness, that the man of God may be
complete, equipped for every good work.*
2 Timothy 3:16–17 esv

If you were to willingly slip on a blindfold, people could easily lead
you astray. You might end up alone on a busy street, or on the
edge of an abyss, or even in another county! That is exactly how
we live when we don't read God's Word. We put on the world's
blinders, and we can be led anywhere. Why? Because we would
be made spiritually vulnerable in many ways. We might plummet
into a pit of temptations and not be able to find a way out. We
might embrace all manner of false teachings because we didn't
know the difference between what is truth and what is a lie.

May we all be on our spiritual toes by reading the Bible,
memorizing the Ten Commandments, and living by the Lord's
precepts. For all scripture is breathed out by God, and it will make
us complete. Then when we get bombarded from all sides, we can
know the truth—God's truth. And that truth promises to set us free.

*Lord, please give me the will and the
discipline to stay in Your Word. Amen.*

Bewitched by Legalisms

O foolish Galatians! Who has bewitched you? It was before your eyes that Jesus Christ was publicly portrayed as crucified. Let me ask you only this: Did you receive the Spirit by works of the law or by hearing with faith?
GALATIANS 3:1–2 ESV

The woman strolled into the chapel—head held high enough to suck in a few mosquitoes. She scowled at the new visitor who sat in her spot! Unfortunately, that frown on her face had long since frozen over like a pond in winter. She had perfected her list of dos and don'ts, but she'd failed to perfect the art of love. She had missed the beauty of Christ altogether, and her joy had drowned in that same icy lake.

Perhaps some people think that the free grace offered in Christ is too nebulous or too good to be true. Whispered lies come to us like, "Legalism is a better grace, because it's concrete and controllable and safe. Legalism doesn't have to get personal or intimate." But our walk with Christ is all about personal and intimate.

Yes, let us always follow the precepts of the Bible, but may we never set up a human-inspired, hyperstrict code of dos and don'ts—sort of a formula to salvation. This approach didn't work for the Pharisees, and it sure won't work for any of us.

Lord, I know as Christians we are no longer under the law. Help me to live fully in Your grace. Amen.

Just Talk to God

God is faithful [He is reliable, trustworthy and ever true to His promise—He can be depended on], and through Him you were called into fellowship with His Son, Jesus Christ our Lord.
1 CORINTHIANS 1:9 AMP

To be honest, you've failed at purging those ugly thoughts about a coworker. Unfortunately, you can't get them out of your head. That woman's brash, overly ambitious, and loudmouthed attitude is like a bulldozer leveling everything in its path—including you! You can't decide if it's time for a loving confrontation or another quiet extension of forgiveness on your part. What now? Talk to God about it.

What about your toddler's terrible twos and your aching back and the lack of time to read your Bible? Talk to God about it. What about your grown kids who refuse to call you and the little chitchats you have with your mother-in-law that invariably disintegrate into a petty free-for-all? Talk to God about it. And what about all your church friends who never seem satisfied with your volunteer work? Well, you know what to do.

No matter what, don't run *from* God. Run *to* Him. He will fold His mighty and compassionate arms around you as you work out this life together. It's the only way to live. It's the only way to joy.

Dearest Lord Jesus, I am riddled with more problems than I can ever handle. Let's talk. Amen.

The Father of Lights

Every good thing given and every perfect gift is from
above; it comes down from the Father of lights [the
Creator and Sustainer of the heavens], in whom there
is no variation [no rising or setting] or shadow cast by
His turning [for He is perfect and never changes].
JAMES 1:17 AMP

When we get real with ourselves, we may finally acknowledge, "In my fury and unforgiveness, I missed the joy and laughter that could have been. In my lust, I found only fleeting pleasures, and then in the process, I forfeited the freedom that I was meant to live. In my selfishness, I lost the blessing that comes with giving. In my haughtiness, I walked away from all that I could be in Christ."

But even then, no matter what, God still loves us and pursues us. Romans 5:8 (NIV) reminds us, "But God demonstrates his own love for us in this: While we were still sinners, Christ died for us." Yes, even while we were in our mess, mercy arrived. We don't deserve it, but God—the Father of lights and the greatest Gift Giver of all time—offered grace to us anyway. But as with any gift, we will need to reach out and accept it.

Thank You, God, for all the many serendipities in this life,
and for the greatest gift of all—Your Son, Jesus Christ. Amen.

Friendships That Go Awry

Cynics look high and low for wisdom—and never find it; the open-minded find it right on their doorstep! Escape quickly from the company of fools; they're a waste of your time, a waste of your words. The wisdom of the wise keeps life on track; the foolishness of fools lands them in the ditch.
PROVERBS 14:6–8 MSG

You're in the ditch again, but you can't figure out why. There's not a lot of light down there. Not much joy either. You have no idea how you got there. How did you fall? Was it from your own error? After much prayer, you realize you're in that emotional ditch because you got shoved into it. By a friend. Again. Oh dear.

Yes, we are to forgive people. But when the fellowship with someone becomes such an ongoing weight that you find yourself almost ill or wanting to hide, that is a good sign you're in need of a healthy break.

A friendship is not the same as making a marriage vow. Of course, friendships should be taken seriously, and they do require work like other relationships. And yet, if that fellowship is always riddled with foolhardiness, misunderstandings, conflict, and strain, it's time to pray for her, love her—but perhaps only from a distance.

Lord, I need You to guide me in all my friendships. Show me when it's time to either set boundaries or gently let them go. Amen.

Truth in Paradox

But grow in the grace and knowledge of our Lord and Savior Jesus Christ. To him be glory both now and forever! Amen.
2 Peter 3:18 niv

Some days you are a fount of love and joy—a real Proverbs 31 woman. You know—"Listen to me roll with biblical thunder, right?" And other days you feel like a big doofus-of-a-saint. The great pretender.

Sometimes we not only give ourselves spiritual mixed messages; at times it appears as though the Bible does too. You may ask, "How can a person be made in the image of God, and be His beloved, if the scriptures also tell us that we're sinners, and all our works are like filthy rags?" There is truth in this paradox—since all of that statement is true. We aren't inherently good people as the world would have us believe, but Christ can change us. In our natural state we're in rebellion with God, and we're headed for destruction. However, we are also meant for redemption in Christ. But we must first embrace the truth of Christ's forgiveness so we—the beloved—can enjoy the second truth of being a new creation.

The growing up of a saint won't happen overnight, but thankfully, God is merciful and God is patient with us.

Lord, I accept Your saving grace so that I can be a child of Yours! Amen.

Passion, Not Obligation

He answered, " 'Love the Lord your God with all your heart and with all your soul and with all your strength and with all your mind'; and, 'Love your neighbor as yourself.' "
LUKE 10:27 NIV

Sometimes that word—*obligation*—can conjure up other words like *coercion*, *force*, and *duress*. These are words that don't generally sound all that joyful. What if everything you did in a relationship came from nothing but guilt? Your attitude would wind down into nothing more than monotonous service and a joyless kind of fellowship. You would become like a little drone, whirring around fulfilling tasks without any emotion or love. There might be lots of well-tuned moving parts—but not a real living soul.

Yes, when we drag ourselves to church and sit in the back with no song in our hearts, when we hurry up with our five minutes of obligatory Bible reading, and when we serve the needy begrudgingly, it feels as though we're missing something huge. Because we are. God doesn't want us to love, worship, or serve Him out of obligation. A love that comes from coercion is no love at all. May we long for and pray for the kind of lavish love that the Lord offers to us freely. Then we can watch as our obligation turns into passion and joy.

Lord, I don't want to just go through the motions, but I want to love You with my whole heart. Amen.

Adrift!

"Then if anyone says to you, 'Look, here is the Christ!' or 'There he is!' do not believe it. For false christs and false prophets will arise and perform great signs and wonders, so as to lead astray, if possible, even the elect. See, I have told you beforehand."
MATTHEW 24:23–25 ESV

There seems to be some real change in America, but it's not always good. Church attendance is down. Suicide is up. Bibles are being pulled out of hotel rooms because people have lost interest. There is a greater fascination with social media maxims than in the precepts of God's Word. We are a nation adrift, and we've gone off course for so long that we've forgotten what land even looks like. We have no anchor. No sails. No true compass to guide us.

We are souls adrift in a joyless sea of transgressions, clinging to a strange half life and latching on to anything that spiritually entices us. All manner of false prophets, teachings, and religions. Also, signs and wonders—some of which are not from God. As well as chasing after people claiming to be Christ. We are warned in the book of Matthew that these days would come. Jesus even said, "See, I have told you beforehand." He was preparing us, and yet too many of us are unprepared. May we all pray hard for our nation and our world. God be with us!

*Oh Lord, may we find our way back to You,
the One and only true God. Amen.*

Reigning Pride

Do nothing from selfishness or empty conceit [through factional motives, or strife], but with [an attitude of] humility [being neither arrogant nor self-righteous], regard others as more important than yourselves. Do not merely look out for your own personal interests, but also for the interests of others.
PHILIPPIANS 2:3–4 AMP

Humans are masters at manipulation. No matter how conceited or aggressive or selfish or self-righteous, or downright slimy our offenses, we can cleverly find a way to blame everyone else but our innocent selves. And we always manage to find a friend who will back us up. What is really going on behind that dark curtain of our denials? Do we think we are too perfect to be accused of anything? Are we too prideful to apologize even when we know we've done wrong?

Christ would rather us err on the side of humility. He would rather us regard others as more important than ourselves. Haughtiness is not only an abomination to God; it will suck all the joy right out of us. May we receive wisdom so we can see our manipulations for what they really are. May we have the courage to denounce them, and the supernatural strength from God to overcome them.

Holy Spirit, I see I have offended someone. I humbly repent. Please forgive me and let me know if I need to go to this person with my apology. Amen.

When to Say No

The apostles returned to Jesus and told him all that they had done and taught. And he said to them, "Come away by yourselves to a desolate place and rest a while." For many were coming and going, and they had no leisure even to eat. And they went away in the boat to a desolate place by themselves.

MARK 6:30–32 ESV

Busyness is quite the thing, isn't it? We love giving the impression that we are valuable people whirling with noble purposes. Doesn't sound too bad, but if we put ourselves in a constant state of "doing," there's a downside called burnout and misery. Wouldn't it be wiser to do two or three things very well and do them with joy than to do five things poorly with an attitude of resentment?

There are many good causes out there, but you don't have to volunteer to do all of them. You might say, "But I can't stand to disappoint people." That's a lovely sentiment, but you still have the right to say no. The enemy would like nothing better than for you to be so exhausted that you lose your zeal, your health, and your joy. Even Jesus and His disciples had to get away from the crowds so they could eat and rest. We need to do the same!

*Holy Spirit, show me when to say
yes and when to say no. Amen.*

A Stranglehold on Your Joy

Be alert and of sober mind. Your enemy the devil prowls
around like a roaring lion looking for someone to devour.
1 PETER 5:8 NIV

Somebody out there must have a perverse and merciless sense
of humor when it comes to female clothing. The fashion tortures
are numerous, but mostly it can be summarized in one word—
pantyhose. You will pull and wiggle, and you will yank and snap.
Of course, all of these actions are painful. And you can forget
about eating anything at a party. These nylon contraptions won't
even let you breathe let alone enjoy a dainty treat! Yes, joy with-
held all in the name of fashion. Fortunately, women are finding
clever ways around this strange custom. Yes, women are smart
enough to know that pantyhose will take the joy right out of life.

On a much more serious note, Satan will try to take the joy
right out of your life too, and he has a thousand and one ways to
do it. The Bible says to be alert and sober-minded. Good advice
when it comes to knowing who can truly put a stranglehold on
your happiness.

Lord, I want to know joy in You. Help me
not to be led astray by the enemy, but may I
always be spiritually watchful and wise. Amen.

The Gift of Joy

"Don't bargain with God. Be direct. Ask for what you need. This isn't a cat-and-mouse, hide-and-seek game we're in. If your child asks for bread, do you trick him with sawdust? If he asks for fish, do you scare him with a live snake on his plate? As bad as you are, you wouldn't think of such a thing. You're at least decent to your own children. So don't you think the God who conceived you in love will be even better?"

MATTHEW 7:7–11 MSG

Have you ever thought something like, *I wonder if God is holding out on me when it comes to my happiness and making my dreams come true?*

God does want us to know happiness, and He does offer us many good gifts throughout our lives. But we could ask ourselves a few questions along the way. For instance, "Do the desires of my heart line up with what is right and good and the will of God?" Or, "Do I expect joyful showers of blessings while I'm busy running away from God in disobedience?" Something to think about as we go before God with our requests.

But God does love us dearly, and He wants to bless us with all good things, including joy!

Lord, I want to be obedient and for my heart desires to line up with Yours! Thank You for Your many good gifts. Amen.

The Book of Joy

Get up, my dear friend, fair and beautiful lover—come to me!
Look around you: Winter is over; the winter rains are over,
gone! Spring flowers are in blossom all over. The whole world's
a choir—and singing! Spring warblers are filling the forest with
sweet arpeggios. Lilacs are exuberantly purple and perfumed,
and cherry trees fragrant with blossoms. Oh, get up, dear
friend, my fair and beautiful lover—come to me! Come, my
shy and modest dove—leave your seclusion, come out in the
open. Let me see your face, let me hear your voice. For
your voice is soothing and your face is ravishing.
Song of Solomon 2:10–14 msg

Ahhh, falling in love. God really knew what He was doing when He created romantic love. And some of that passionate rapture is exquisitely presented in the Song of Solomon. These scriptures are also a beautiful reflection on how our God truly loves His people. Oh, to be cherished so dearly by our creator God!

So, if you haven't read the Song of Solomon lately, you might want to once again experience this book filled with joy. It'll make your soul rise up like blossoms in springtime.

Creator God, thank You for providing such endearing
writings on romance. I love reading Your holy Word.
It makes my heart sing! In Jesus' name I pray, amen.

A Test

The Israelites did as they were told; some gathered much, some little. And when they measured it by the omer, the one who gathered much did not have too much, and the one who gathered little did not have too little. Everyone had gathered just as much as they needed. Then Moses said to them, "No one is to keep any of it until morning." However, some of them paid no attention to Moses; they kept part of it until morning, but it was full of maggots and began to smell. So Moses was angry with them.

EXODUS 16:17–20 NIV

When your kids make a running leap into your arms without a care, that proves they trust in you and your love for them.

God tested the Israelites with His manna from heaven to see if they fully trusted Him. Some of the Israelites failed. They gathered more manna than they could eat in one day. God didn't want His people stockpiling food to give them a feeling of human security—with the idea that they could go it alone if God failed them. The Lord wanted their complete trust—that He could take care of them, which He faithfully did in spite of their disbelief and groanings. But God's test wasn't just one of faith—it was also a test of love.

Do we pass the test?

Lord, I know You have proven Yourself to be faithful. May I always trust You for every detail of my life. Amen.

When the Kids Are Busy

*Inside the tent the Lord spoke to Moses face-to-face,
as a man speaks to his friend. Afterwards Moses would
return to the camp, but the young man who assisted him,
Joshua (son of Nun), stayed behind in the Tabernacle.*

EXODUS 33:11 TLB

The older widow sat by the phone. Since it was her birthday, she thought that her kids would surely call. So she waited patiently. No presents had arrived, but that didn't matter since just talking to her kids was one of the greatest joys of her life. She knew they were busy with their own lives now. Yes, a lot going on with work and the kids and church. She knew they loved her, oh yes, but sometimes she did wish there was more of "a showing" of that love and not just "a saying" of it.

Nighttime arrived and the older woman reluctantly gave up her seat by the phone. She sighed a deep longing kind of sigh, but she went to bed with hope, still loving her kids and believing they would surely call tomorrow. . . .

*Jesus, is that a little how it feels to You when Your kids don't
want to talk to You? I'm so sorry, Lord, for all the times I've
been too busy for You. I love You. Let's talk now. Amen.*

A Divine Forgetfulness

Anyone who claims to be in the light but hates a brother or sister is still in the darkness. Anyone who loves their brother and sister lives in the light, and there is nothing in them to make them stumble. But anyone who hates a brother or sister is in the darkness and walks around in the darkness. They do not know where they are going, because the darkness has blinded them.

1 JOHN 2:9–11 NIV

Yeah, sometimes people do things that drive us crazy. They wound us and then make it look like it's our fault. The injustice! We fume. We rant. We lose sleep. And then as Christians, we realize we can't live that way, so we try to forgive them. But sometimes it doesn't seem to take. Our minds bring up the offense over and over.

So we pray for them. Yes, it is indeed hard to pray for someone while harboring ill feelings. And in those continuing acts of obedience to God, we step out of the darkness and into the light of forgiveness. Yes, we can move on in love, even if it only starts with a trickle. After all, since Christ offers us what we could tenderly call a "divine forgetfulness" when it comes to *our* transgressions, it is right and good that we offer the same thing to others.

Lord, when it comes to the offenses against me, may I grow to have more of Your "divine forgetfulness." Amen.

The Light of Life

*Again Jesus spoke to them, saying, "I am the light
of the world. Whoever follows me will not walk
in darkness, but will have the light of life."*
JOHN 8:12 ESV

The woman knew little about art except for what she loved—like the mystifying smile of Mona Lisa and the statue of David, Michelangelo's masterpiece. Some of the paintings that made her heart ache with joy depicted objects illuminated against a dark background. Perhaps there was the rich sheen of a brass pot, the glistening of a goblet, the soft glow on clusters of grapes, or a face lit by some unseen radiant light.

That light, she thought, made all the difference on the canvas, changing every single object it touched. In fact, that light was the life of the painting.

That is just the way Christ lights us up and changes us if we allow Him to. Jesus said, "I am the light of the world. Whoever follows me will not walk in darkness, but will have the light of life."

In a way, we are like living art, and our lives will never have true beauty and joy without the light of Christ. May we pray for the light—His light!

Thank You, Lord, for filling my life with Your light. Amen.

Keep Flowing

"After removing Saul, he made David their king. God testified concerning him: 'I have found David son of Jesse, a man after my own heart; he will do everything I want him to do.' "
ACTS 13:22 NIV

King David is known as a man after God's own heart. David was faithful, humble, and he loved God, and yet he was a flawed hero. Remember Bathsheba? But King David kept serving God.

Sometimes we get into a mind-set that we shouldn't move forward in life until our motivations are flawless. We might say, "Unless I can give perfectly, do perfectly, I will give and do nothing at all." Yes, and the enemy would like nothing better than for us to be trapped in a spiritual holding pattern. Even though Christ is indeed perfecting us and making us more into His likeness day by day, Christians will not be absolutely perfect on this side of eternity. Even King David was far from perfect. But it didn't stop him from dancing before God. It didn't stop him from offering himself up time and time again to the service of God. It didn't stop him from becoming one of the greatest biblical heroes of all time.

Flawed vessels might have a few blemishes, but with God's help, a weak vessel can still flow with life-giving water.

Lord, as You make me more and more into Your likeness, help me to keep working for Your kingdom. Amen.

Little Lamb

*If we confess our sins, he is faithful and just and will
forgive us our sins and purify us from all unrighteousness.*
1 JOHN 1:9 NIV

The father went to his daughter—whom he'd nicknamed Little
Lamb—and asked her if she had eaten the rest of the cookies in
the jar. The little girl hesitated, but the look of love on her daddy's
face was so real she knew she was safe in his love. The little girl
nodded with tears of repentance. The father forgave his Little
Lamb, and he wrapped his arms around her. He stayed with her
during her tummy ache until she was all ready to run out and play
again. The girl loved the way her daddy loved her, and she never
raided that cookie jar again.

To ask God to forgive us, well, it's as easy as the story of that
loving dad and his little girl. Why can't we see how accessible
forgiveness is? Why can't we see that adoring love on the Lord's
face? Shouldn't it always melt our hearts in tender submission?

May our adult pride be ever transformed into the simple faith
of a child. And then we can go back out and do life, with a lighter
step and a joyful smile.

I praise You, Lord, for Your mercies and forgiveness! Amen.

Take a Joy Break

You make known to me the path of life; in your presence there is fullness of joy; at your right hand are pleasures forevermore.
PSALM 16:11 ESV

The minister-counselor listened patiently to his parishioner, and after hearing a long list of complaints and woes, he counseled her, prayed with her, and then wrote out something that looked like a doctor's prescription. The note read, "Take one joy break every day or as often as needed." Okay, so what is a joy break?

God wants us to enjoy this life. So take time to pause over the fullness of joy found in His presence as well as the many pleasures He provides. How about a few of these?

Take in the breathless wonder of diamond stars strewn across a black velvet sky.

Check out the world's tiniest bird online—the bee humming-bird in all its bejeweled glory.

Rejoice when you witness the miracle of sorrow transformed into joy.

Feel the cooling mist off the thundering crash of ocean waves.

Come to know the sweet forgiveness between friends.

Watch an inspired mind at work in the wondrous act of creation.

You can make your own joy list. And don't forget to take one daily or as often as needed!

Lord, thank You for Your radiant presence, Your miracles, and Your many creative wonders. I am in awe of You! Amen.

A Close Encounter

"If you abide in me, and my words abide in you, ask whatever you wish, and it will be done for you. By this my Father is glorified, that you bear much fruit and so prove to be my disciples. As the Father has loved me, so have I loved you. Abide in my love. If you keep my commandments, you will abide in my love, just as I have kept my Father's commandments and abide in his love. These things I have spoken to you, that my joy may be in you, and that your joy may be full."

JOHN 15:7–11 ESV

There is a cynical haze covering our earth that's more serious than pollution—it is a poisonous cloud of spiritual apathy. That is, an indifference to Christ and His precepts, as well as a cynical view of His church.

We have drifted far away from what the Lord asks of us—and that is to abide in His love, keep His commandments, and bear much fruit.

We need to have a close encounter with God. We need the saving grace of Christ Jesus. In the book of John, we see such a beautiful explanation of the closeness we are longing for. May we not only tuck these verses in our hearts but live them daily. For abiding in the Lord's love is knowing real joy.

Lord, our world needs a close encounter with You. Amen.

Going It Alone

*God makes a home for the lonely; He leads the
prisoners into prosperity, only the stubborn
and rebellious dwell in a parched land.*
PSALM 68:6 AMP

The day arrives when you have to say goodbye to your child. College is over, and now a new level of empty nest has arrived. You expect the usual goodbye scene with tender tears and hugs and promises to stay in touch. But your young man surprises you—shocks you really—by saying that while he appreciates it that you created him, he really wants to go it alone now. Also, he doesn't think he'll contact you again. Well, unless something goes terribly wrong and he needs you for money or something.

Oh. You feel like dying right there in the street from the pain of those words. Will your son ever return home again? Will he ever love you? Will he live a life of rebellion?

Isn't that a bit similar to the way some of us act when we try to go it alone without God? We might acknowledge His existence, but we don't feel a need for an ongoing relationship. Do know—we weren't meant for a parched, lonely, and independent life. We were meant to fellowship with the One true God who loved us enough to not only create us but to redeem us when *we* went terribly wrong.

*Lord, forgive me for acting like I can do life
without You. I love You, and I need You! Amen.*

Where I Am Headed

Yet what we suffer now is nothing compared
to the glory he will give us later.
ROMANS 8:18 TLB

You've known physical pain or depression or sorrow for some time now—but the people around you seem to be walking on air. You may scream, "Where is my God? Where are my answers? Where is the joy?"

The suffering in this life can be sudden, unrelenting, and grueling. So what can be done? What happens when our questions, yearnings, and petitions are met with silence?

Keep on praying. And as you wait on God, take comfort in knowing you are not alone. Christ suffered beyond all our human imaginings, and He promises never to leave us or forsake us. As Christians, there is also joy in knowing where we are headed at the appointed time by God. To heaven. To glory. By the Lord's side forever, unfettered and no longer broken. This life is only a mere flash compared to the boundless time of eternity.

In moments of great trial, think on these things.

Father God, I am at the point of breaking from
all my pain. Please come to me now and help
me. If I am to wait for healing, please send Your
Comforter, and may I never forget the joyful place
I am headed one day. In Jesus' name I pray, amen.

Sprinklers of Serendipities

Watch the way you talk. Let nothing foul or dirty come out of your mouth. Say only what helps, each word a gift.
EPHESIANS 4:29 MSG

The wee lassie loved to dress up as a princess—as most young girls like to do—and so she went around sprinkling folks with her little pink wand, which was loaded with pixie dust. Of course, adoring grandparents played along, pretending to be transformed into pure joy when she gave them a dusting of the sparkly stuff. Everyone smiled and laughed and hugged. Such fun.

As Christians we don't pepper people with pixie dust, but we do have the joy of the Lord we can share with folks. May we choose to live a life of encouragement. It costs us nothing. It only takes a moment to turn a frown upside down. May we all choose not to be the messengers of little miseries, but instead may we choose to be sprinklers of serendipities. May we spread the hope of Christ and the joy of salvation. May each of our words be a gift. We have a choice. Choose wisely.

Dear God, may I use my words to help people. May I see them as gifts used for encouragement. In Jesus' name I pray, amen.

The Joy of Sharing

"If you have two coats, give one away," he said.
"Do the same with your food."
LUKE 3:11 MSG

You open the fridge and there it is—two leftover slices of chocolate cake with buttercream frosting. Ohhh, so rich and gooey and chocolatey. That leftover cake sits there like a beacon on a hill representing all things beautiful and delicious. You cannot resist. Both pieces are calling your name. But wait.

You know your husband has had a long, rough day, and he was dreaming of that cake too. If you ate both pieces, you would most likely get a bellyache. But even if you didn't get overly full, you would miss the look of joy on your husband's face as he dug into that delicious treat.

God wants us to have a generous heart. As we share what we have with others, we share in their joy too.

Father God, sometimes when I see people in need,
I can come up with a million excuses why I deserve to
keep all my money rather than sharing what I have.
Show me how to give wisely to those who really need
my help. And may I have compassion and love for all
people just like You do. In Jesus' name I pray, amen.

Living Lightly

"Are you tired? Worn out? Burned out on religion? Come to me. Get away with me and you'll recover your life. I'll show you how to take a real rest. Walk with me and work with me—watch how I do it. Learn the unforced rhythms of grace. I won't lay anything heavy or ill-fitting on you. Keep company with me and you'll learn to live freely and lightly."
MATTHEW 11:28–30 MSG

The joy had long since gone out of the woman's beautiful green eyes. She looked in the mirror and knew too well it was going to be another long, miserable day. But what was wrong?

She'd lost sleep, worrying about her kids in college. Her new diet had failed. Her stepfather was coming to town and she wasn't sure how the visit would go. And she knew at work that she was a breath away from getting laid off. Wow, that *is* a lot to deal with. But as a Christian, why would she deliberately carry those heavy burdens? Simply put—she didn't totally trust God with the details of her life. And yet the Lord promises us that His yoke is easy and His burden is light. Let us all go away with the Lord, truly rest in Him, and recover our lives again. May we keep such close company with Him that we can learn how to live freely and lightly!

Holy Spirit, please show me how to trust You with the big stuff in my life, and the little stuff. Amen.

Let There Be Life!

Oh yes, you shaped me first inside, then out;
you formed me in my mother's womb. I thank you,
High God—you're breathtaking! Body and soul,
I am marvelously made! I worship in adoration—
what a creation! You know me inside and out, you
know every bone in my body; you know exactly
how I was made, bit by bit, how I was sculpted from
nothing into something. Like an open book, you
watched me grow from conception to birth; all the
stages of my life were spread out before you, the days
of my life all prepared before I'd even lived one day.
PSALM 139:13–16 MSG

God is a lover of life. And He watched you grow from conception to birth. All the stages of your life were spread out before you.

Anytime we lessen the sacredness of our babes in the womb, we lessen our dignity. Every child, no matter how tiny or sickly or ill timed, is innocent and precious. And yet each child is vulnerable to our government policies, our cultural mores, and our errant whims. May we never forget that we've been given a holy calling to watch over them, nourish them, and cherish them, for every one of these babes is not just full of life—they are eternal beings with the divine imprint of God Himself.

Lord, may we as a people, nation,
and world celebrate life like You do. Amen.

What Is Victorious

*"He loads the thick cloud with moisture; the clouds
scatter his lightning. They turn round and round by his
guidance, to accomplish all that he commands them
on the face of the habitable world. Whether for correction,
or for his land, or for love, he causes it to happen."*
JOB 37:11–13 NRSV

Have you ever been on a destructive kind of roll, and then you
couldn't quite stop? Say, you run a red light and then decide to
drive away even faster. Maybe you're thinking, *Well, I've already
broken the law once and gotten away with it, so what does a little
speeding matter.* But if you continue with that mentality, you're
going to end up with a ticket or in an accident or maybe even in
jail. The enemy would like to keep us in a mode of haplessness
and haughtiness so we'll spiral out of control.

But the Lord can give us the supernatural power to stop. He
will help us flee from the enemy and his many deceitful and twisted
mind games. If God can command the lightning, the thunder, and
all of nature, then He can take our lives from what can be injurious
to what will be victorious. Just ask.

---

*Lord, please forgive me and help me to find
my way back into Your presence and joy. Amen.*

Awakenings to a New Life

Therefore if anyone is in Christ [that is, grafted in, joined to Him by faith in Him as Savior], he is a new creature [reborn and renewed by the Holy Spirit]; the old things [the previous moral and spiritual condition] have passed away. Behold, new things have come [because spiritual awakening brings a new life].

2 CORINTHIANS 5:17 AMP

You pull out a shabby old coat from your closet to see if there is any good left in it. But there are thinnish places here and there where you can see through the fabric. The lining is stained. And one of the pockets is just about to fall off. You want to fix it, but the coat has got to go. Then you buy a brand-new coat and slip it on. Oh, how wonderful. The old coat has passed away. Behold, the new coat has come. And you are so grateful. You want to shout. But you're in the middle of a crowd at the mall, and so you hold on to your joy until you're in your car. Then you snuggle into the warmth of your new jacket and thank God for His generosity.

So, if replacing a beater coat with a beautiful new one can feel so good, imagine being reborn into a whole new person!

*Thank You, Lord, for giving me a spiritual awakening.
It has brought me new life and joy! Amen.*

How Are We to Live?

Pride goes before destruction,
a haughty spirit before a fall.
PROVERBS 16:18 NIV

Pride is as common as watching the sun come up—only it's not at all beautiful to behold. Pride is a sin and comes before destruction. In fact, pride was behind man's original sin in the garden of Eden.

To keep ourselves far from arrogance, then, we might be tempted to swing too far the other way into false pride. Perhaps you've said, "I have no talent. I'm not attractive. Oh, me and my failures. Me and my stupidity." And on and on. But there is still some "I" and "me" in that hot mess of self-flagellation. Perhaps you really *do* believe you're inferior to all humankind. But even then, when we are constantly putting ourselves down we are not lifting up God, since He made us in His likeness.

How are we to live then? We need to know who we are in Christ. Precious but fallen. Saved but we are not the Savior. We have talents and gifts, yes, but they are to be used for God's glory and our shared pleasure with Him, not a private struggle toward fame.

In the confines of biblical living we will find true freedom. And in that freedom will reside true joy.

Lord Jesus, may I run from pride and
live just as You created me to live. Amen.

His Dwelling Place

*Now it happened that when the priests had come out
of the Holy Place, the cloud filled the LORD's house,
so the priests could not stand [in their positions] to
minister because of the cloud, for the glory and brilliance
of the LORD had filled the LORD's house (temple). Then
Solomon said, "The LORD has said that He would dwell
in the thick darkness [of the cloud]. I have certainly built
You a lofty house, a place for You to dwell in forever."*
1 KINGS 8:10–13 AMP

Imagine that scene in 1 Kings—the brilliant presence of the Lord
filling the temple. What a glorious moment in time. The hearts
of the Israelites surely must have skipped a few beats as they
stumbled back in pure awe.

Yes, Solomon made a dwelling place for God, and it was
truly beautiful. Now Christ has come, and He left us with His
Holy Spirit. As Christians, we are a dwelling place for God—we
house His presence in our innermost being. As it reminds us in
1 Corinthians 6:19–20 (NRSV), "Or do you not know that your body
is a temple of the Holy Spirit within you, which you have from
God, and that you are not your own? For you were bought with
a price; therefore glorify God in your body."

May the world see that radiant glow of the Lord's presence
in us every day!

*Lord, may I be a beautiful dwelling
place for Your Holy Spirit. Amen.*

A Joyful Place to Be

*And so, dear brothers and sisters, I plead with you to give
your bodies to God because of all he has done for you.
Let them be a living and holy sacrifice—the kind he will
find acceptable. This is truly the way to worship him.*
ROMANS 12:1 NLT

You're a Christ follower, but sometimes, do you still feel like you
are missing something valuable? Like joy?

If you are in need of this treasure of the soul, then this prayer
will help. "Oh Lord, even though I have accepted You as my Lord
and Savior, I feel that I haven't surrendered everything to You. I'm
still clutching on to pieces of my life, and like a child, sometimes I
still demand my own way. But my ways are not working. I am truly
ready to say, 'I have come to the end of me and my own faulty
wisdom. I would rather please You, Lord, than please myself. I
surrender all of me into Your hands. May I be a living and holy
sacrifice to You.'"

Yes, in that total surrender to the Lord there is peace and joy
to be found.

---

*Almighty God, I yield myself to Your will. Mold me
into something beautiful and usable for Your
kingdom. In Jesus' name I pray, amen.*

David's Choice

"Go and tell David, 'This is what the LORD says: I am giving you three options. Choose one of them for me to carry out against you.'" So Gad went to David and said to him, "Shall there come on you three years of famine in your land? Or three months of fleeing from your enemies while they pursue you? Or three days of plague in your land? Now then, think it over and decide how I should answer the one who sent me." David said to Gad, "I am in deep distress. Let us fall into the hands of the LORD, for his mercy is great; but do not let me fall into human hands."
2 SAMUEL 24:12–14 NIV

In 2 Samuel we discover that King David sinned before God by having a census created. This request on David's part may have been perceived as prideful as well as a reliance on his own strength and not on the power of the Lord.

God then gave David a choice of three serious punishments. David chose not to fall into human hands because he trusted God more than he trusted man. David knew that God loved him and that He was full of mercy as well as justice.

Yes, even when we've sinned before God and we have to face the consequences with a sharp reproof, it will always be better than falling into the hands of the world or the enemy.

Lord, I trust You, even when I need to be admonished for my folly. Amen.

The Simple Things

The LORD will indeed give what is good,
and our land will yield its harvest.
PSALM 85:12 NIV

Sometimes while we're waiting on life's big majestic joys to come along, we miss the little beauties that pop up here and there. But the smallish things can also soften a hard day and gladden many a heavy heart. Here is just a smattering of blessings we might overlook: the sweet and mellow fragrance of pears and apples at harvesttime, the laughter between old friends, the gurgling coos of a newborn babe, the running of the deer through the meadow, a new pair of woolly socks on a chilly day, the merry leap of a frog into a misty pond, a sunset so ablaze with color that it seems to be hand-painted by heaven itself, the smiles all around from a job well done, or a wildflower-picking day with the kids.

Yes, the Lord will indeed give us what is good and lovely. May we always be thankful for our many blessings. We could even write them down in a little journal, and then from time to time, we could let the remembrance of them bring us great joy.

Father God, I love all the little beauties that
You sprinkle throughout my day. May I not
miss a single one. In Jesus' name I pray, amen.

This Beautiful Blue Planet

*And God blessed them [granting them certain authority]
and said to them, "Be fruitful, multiply, and fill the earth,
and subjugate it [putting it under your power]; and rule
over (dominate) the fish of the sea, the birds of the air,
and every living thing that moves upon the earth."*
GENESIS 1:28 AMP

There is that wild patch of brambles on your property, and something is calling you to it. You can't quite put your finger on it, but you have this yearning to tidy it and make it into a park—a tiny bit of Eden. You might find a hidden vineyard there in the thicket or perhaps some ferns that look primeval. Or maybe you'll discover some trees of a rare variety that just need some tending and some sunlight so they can thrive again. And so you do it. And what was once chaos is now subdued into a thing of beauty and joy!

Yes, God's calling to us to be guardians of this beautiful planet is real and far from frivolous. However, the Lord has never called us to worship creation as some are doing—which is idolatry. We are instead called to be caretakers of God's beautiful earth. What a huge responsibility, but oh, such a great honor.

*Oh Lord, show us how to watch
over Your world with care. Amen.*

Disenchantment

God, my shepherd! I don't need a thing. You have
bedded me down in lush meadows, you find me
quiet pools to drink from. True to your word, you let
me catch my breath and send me in the right direction.
PSALM 23:1–3 MSG

It would be impossible for us not to feel some serious disenchantment from time to time over the state of world affairs, the plight of humanity, and our own spiritual frailties. But God remains true to us no matter what. He is our Shepherd, and we are His beloved sheep. He wants to refresh and restore us. If we let Him, the Lord will lead us by quiet pools of water and lush meadows. Don't you love that? Everyone could benefit from strolling along a stream and then resting on sumptuous grasses. The velvety kind that always comes up in the springtime and always seems to be hiding a nest of baby bunnies!

Take the time to breathe the fresh air and to watch the butterflies dancing through the field. Listen to the breeze as it passes through the wildflowers. Yes, enjoy God's creation. He will walk with you and talk to you. Let Him take your disenchantment and turn it into delight—for abiding in His company is everything we need for a life of joy.

Lord Jesus, lead me beside quiet pools of water
and lush grasses. I am ready to be restored! Amen.

In Jesus' Name I Pray

And God spoke all these words, saying, "I am the LORD your God, who brought you out of the land of Egypt, out of the house of slavery. You shall have no other gods before me."

EXODUS 20:1–3 ESV

If you look online for health tips, you'll find a plethora of ways to stay young and healthy and vibrant. Everybody seems to want to roll back the clock these days. Sometimes you'll find "prayer" on the list of ideas for wellness, and sometimes the articles don't specify whom you are to pray to. They think that pretty much any god or even the universe will do. But that counsel is in direct opposition to one of the Ten Commandments in the Bible, which states, "You shall have no other gods before me." That is as clear as it gets. We are not to commune with or beseech or delight in any other gods.

Make sure you're praying to the One who sacrificed His life for you. The One—Jesus—who rose again so you could be offered eternal life. No other god can make that claim of power and love.

Dear God, I pray to You and only You. May I never be enticed by false religions or the spiritual forces of evil in the heavenly places. In Jesus' holy name I pray, amen.

That Stinging Pinch of Judgment

*"Stop judging by mere appearances,
but instead judge correctly."*
JOHN 7:24 NIV

You've got this pair of shiny new stiletto heels that are the coolest thing, right? But after fifteen to thirty minutes, all your chic style has morphed into feet on fire! Then the bulbous blisters arrive along with the throbbing pain. The fashion fun is so over. Back to your mud-green clogs.

Mmmm. The whole scene sort of reminds you of a friend of yours. You meet up for lunch and hug. You chitchat. You laugh a little and loosen up some more. The friendship is feeling pretty good. But about fifteen to thirty minutes later, the joy is over. You're feeling that pinch—only this time it's the pinch that comes from judgment. Before you can even fully explain your joke or your unique wording or your action—well, your friend has donned that sanctimonious look of a swift verdict. Yes, she has officially sized you up, judged you, and condemned you to some gloomy abyss somewhere. And you haven't even had time for dessert yet!

Lord, please help me not to be the friend who condemns people with unfair judgment, but may Your divine wisdom guide me in all my reasonings and all my speech. Amen.

Doubt

*Now when John [the Baptist] in prison heard about the
activities of Christ, he sent word by his disciples and asked
Him, "Are You the Expected One (the Messiah), or should
we look for someone else [who will be the promised One]?"
Jesus answered, "Go and report to John what you hear and
see: the blind receive [their] sight and the lame walk, the
lepers are cleansed [by healing] and the deaf hear, the dead
are raised, and the poor have the gospel preached to them.
And blessed [joyful, favored by God] is he who does not
take offense at Me [accepting Me as the Messiah and
trusting confidently in My message of salvation]."*
MATTHEW 11:2–6 AMP

The roar of a tornado is upon you as you hunker down in the
closet. Fear seizes you. You pray hard. Then a niggling doubt
comes: *What if no one is really there to hear my prayer?*

In Matthew we see that John the Baptist—a true biblical
hero—had a moment of questioning too. While in prison he
wanted to make certain Jesus was really who He said He was. A
reassuring answer came back to John, and he surely must have
died with confidence, knowing he had spoken the truth—that
Jesus was, in fact, the long-awaited Messiah. When you are riddled with terrors and doubts, take heart. We too can know the
same confidence as John.

*Lord, thank You for giving us the joy-filled assurance
in Your Word that You are the Messiah. Amen.*

What Little I Have

One of his disciples, Andrew, Simon Peter's brother, said to
him, "There is a boy here who has five barley loaves and two
fish, but what are they for so many?" Jesus said, "Have the
people sit down." Now there was much grass in the place.
So the men sat down, about five thousand in number.
Jesus then took the loaves, and when he had given thanks,
he distributed them to those who were seated. So also
the fish, as much as they wanted.

JOHN 6:8–11 ESV

Bella always felt a little shabby and inadequate in life. She had
no business acumen, degrees, wealth, or unique achievements
to speak of. She couldn't even dazzle anyone with witty conversation at a gathering of friends. But one day someone encouraged
Bella—telling her that she had the gift of servanthood.

Just like the little boy in the Bible who offered his simple gift
of the loaves and fishes to Jesus, Bella gave what she had to the
Lord. And just as the boy witnessed a miracle that day when Jesus
fed the multitude with his meager lunch, so did Bella come to
see miracles. Time and time again, she saw how a simple giving
from the heart could be magnified and exalted for the Lord's use.
Yes, may all our many gifts of every kind come to glorify God!

Lord, what I have may be small, but it's Yours.
Please bless my gift for Your holy use. Amen.

The Kiddie Car

*The king's heart is like a stream of water directed
by the Lord; he guides it wherever he pleases.*
PROVERBS 21:1 NLT

There once was a little girl who loved going to the grocery store with her mom. She'd sit in the plastic car that was connected to the front of the shopping cart, and she'd steer with all her might. As the little girl grew up, she saw that the control panel and steering wheel were hooked up to nothing at all. The truth was she had been merely pretending to maneuver around the store. All her control was no more than an illusion.

And so it goes with us when we try to take complete control of our little universe. At times, we get power hungry and too domineering as a mother, volunteer, friend, spouse, parishioner, consumer, and citizen. We wake up knowing that we can steer our way through all areas of our lives, and we can know the outcome of all things. But in the end, we don't have a whole lot more control of this world than the little girl in the plastic car.

God is in control, and He is the only One who should be. After all, He is the One who made us, watches over us, and loves us best. We should pray, of course, but also know that the ultimate controls are in the hands of God.

*Lord, I acknowledge and welcome Your
divine control. In fact, I find joy in it! Amen.*

He'll Quiet You with His Love

"The LORD *your God is in your midst, a mighty one who will save; he will rejoice over you with gladness; he will quiet you by his love; he will exult over you with loud singing."*
ZEPHANIAH 3:17 ESV

The mother rocked her newborn back and forth. Back and forth. Her infant was so precious, tiny, and vulnerable—everything within her wanted to protect her baby from harm and to love him forever. When the wee one wriggled and fussed the mom held him closer and whispered, "Shhh, my little one. I'm here. All is well." The mother kissed her boy ever so tenderly. This young mother couldn't imagine ever being parted from her beloved. Her child was her life. Her joy.

The Lord God loves us in the same way. When we are distressed or weary in this life, may we look to the Lord. He will come near and quiet us with His love. He will rejoice over us with gladness. He will exalt over us with loud singing. Imagine. The Creator of the universe. Love like that—for me, for you!

I praise You, Almighty God, for Your love hems me in, and it restores my soul. I love You with all my heart! In Jesus' name I pray, amen.

A Time to Share

Offer hospitality to one another without grumbling.
1 PETER 4:9 NIV

The woman had been collecting pretty dishes since forever, until her kitchen and dining room cabinets couldn't hold one more piece. She decided to count the incredible array of dishes, serving trays, cutlery, and tea things. Wow, pretty staggering. She had certainly been busy buying! And yet there it all sat, unused and unenjoyed. The sight suddenly didn't seem happy. To own it all felt more burdensome than blissful. What had been her reasoning? she wondered. Had she not wanted to take the time to share what she had with others? Did she worry people would chip her beautiful dishes? But wouldn't risking a chip or two be better than hiding such beauties?

Perhaps the Holy Spirit had given her a divine nudge. Yes, indeed, and she intended to take action. She opened up her home for all kinds of gatherings—luncheons, Bible studies, neighborhood meet-and-greets, tea parties, Christmas gift exchanges, baby showers, and even a small wedding. Oh, how life had changed. She had discovered that the joy wasn't so much in the buying and collecting but in the sharing!

Lord, thank You for blessing me so that I can bless others. I want to show people hospitality, and I want to do it with a cheerful heart. Amen.

A Circle of Love

Then turning toward the woman he said to Simon, "Do you see this woman? I entered your house; you gave me no water for my feet, but she has wet my feet with her tears and wiped them with her hair. You gave me no kiss, but from the time I came in she has not ceased to kiss my feet."
LUKE 7:44–45 ESV

Many people know John 3:16 by heart, but do they love God in return with all their heart? Love is meant to be a circle—like the warming confines of a mutual hug.

We see in Luke 7 that Jesus deeply appreciated the love shown by this repentant woman at Simon's house. You will also find scriptures throughout the Bible that speak on this issue of loving God. The Lord deserves our love—He is worthy of it. And yet the Lord wants our love to be genuine, coming from a place of freedom and spontaneity. These are the same hopes we have when we enter into relationships on earth. God doesn't want a robotic acquiescence, which is no love at all. This is why humans were given free will, so that when we do fall in love with God, it is real and joyful and all it's meant to be.

Lord, I want to love You more.
Please show me how. Amen.

Chasing the Wind

I, the Preacher, have been king over Israel in Jerusalem. And I set my mind to seek and explore by [man's] wisdom all [human activity] that has been done under heaven. It is a miserable business and a burdensome task which God has given the sons of men with which to be busy and distressed. I have seen all the works which have been done under the sun, and behold, all is vanity, a futile grasping and chasing after the wind.

ECCLESIASTES 1:12–14 AMP

There is some disagreement among scholars as to the author of Ecclesiastes, but if the writer was indeed King Solomon, we know that at times he possessed extraordinary wisdom and a devotion to God, but at other times he committed wicked deeds and lived what could easily be called a "chasing after the wind."

If we make an honest assessment of our lives, how are we doing with our human activity? Do we love God more than the things of the world, or are we busy chasing after what we see the world chasing after? And have we allowed our "chasing" to deteriorate further into addictions, decadence, greed, or vanity?

May we discover all the wisdom that Ecclesiastes has to offer, and may we grow up into godly women whose lives are filled with real meaning and real joy!

Holy Spirit, enlighten me as I read this unique book of the Bible—Ecclesiastes. Amen.

Our Place in God's Family

*"You're blessed when you can show people how to cooperate
instead of compete or fight. That's when you discover
who you really are, and your place in God's family."*
MATTHEW 5:9 MSG

Oh dear. The kids at recess were at it again. No one wanted to take turns on the swings. It was a brand-new piece of equipment on the playground, and of course, it suddenly had to be everyone's favorite. Several kids bickered over that last empty swing. Quickly, little June stepped in and showed them the joys of taking turns, and with a little coaxing, they finally went along with her idea. June had wisely learned at a young age that life went more smoothly when she shared and when she helped her friends to get along. Before intervening, the teachers had often seen June in action and admired the tenderness and tenacity of her peacemaking gifts.

Is that how we play in our adult world? Do we share what we have with others? Do we choose to make the world *less* competitive and combative and *more* peaceful and godly? Have we found our place in God's family?

*Father God, in a world filled with war and violence and
hate-filled speech, please make me an ambassador of Your
love and peace and joy. In Jesus' holy name I pray, amen.*

To Have Purpose Is to Have Joy

*Don't you remember the rule we had when we lived with you?
"If you don't work, you don't eat." And now we're getting
reports that a bunch of lazy good-for-nothings are taking
advantage of you. This must not be tolerated. We command them
to get to work immediately—no excuses, no arguments—and
earn their own keep. Friends, don't slack off in doing your duty.*
2 THESSALONIANS 3:10–13 MSG

There are a zillion and one reasons *not* to go to work, but there is one big reason to go anyway—God wants us to. *Oh, that.* We could come up with some excuses like, "This menial work I'm doing is not really my calling." Or, "I am not appreciated enough or paid enough at my job." Or, "I am destined for a real career, not a mere job." Or, "I'd rather chase fun pursuits and pleasures than work a real job." The list can be long, but the short truth is, in order to do what is right, we need to work. The Lord says in His Word that we should not eat if we do not work. Good honest work will help us rise in the morning with hope, and it will also give us a more satisfying slumber at night.

To have purpose is to have joy.

*Lord, please show me what my purpose is, and until
then, may I always be willing to work. Amen.*

Our Many Acts of Worship

Wearing a linen ephod, David was dancing before the Lord
with all his might, while he and all Israel were bringing up
the ark of the Lord with shouts and the sound of trumpets.
As the ark of the Lord was entering the City of David,
Michal daughter of Saul watched from a window.
And when she saw King David leaping and dancing
before the Lord, she despised him in her heart.
2 Samuel 6:14–16 niv

The Bible offers us some really beautiful accounts of worship. There's the story of the woman who poured her costly perfume onto the feet of Christ. We read about David dancing before the Lord. And we discover the poor widow giving all she had to God. All of these are such deeply meaningful acts of worship.

What can you do to adore and praise God for who He is and all He's doing in your life? Perhaps during your morning Bible time you could sing a new song before the Lord. Maybe you could befriend someone at work who's friendless. Or perhaps on cold winter days you could hand out blankets to the needy. What will your worship look like today?

Dear God, I want to worship You in all the ways
that will bring You honor and joy. For Your joy
is my joy! In Jesus' name I pray, amen.

When You Need a Rescue

The LORD is close to the brokenhearted
and saves those who are crushed in spirit.
PSALM 34:18 NIV

Some days, the joy simply does not come. You pray for it. You crave it. You imagine it. You surround yourself with upbeat Christians. You stay busy and focus on the needs of others. You read the Word. But the joy still seems to elude you. And you still find yourself lonely, depressed, and broken. Now what?

The Old Testament is full of stories, showing people in the throes of all kinds of heartaches. And even in the time of Christ, there was much suffering. In fact, even though Jesus knew joy, the scriptures do not refer to Him as a man of high spirits. Jesus was known more for His power, love, healing, forgiveness, friendship, sacrifice, and resurrection. So when you feel broken and crushed in spirit, take heart. The Lord knows your suffering. The Lord loves you. Talk to Him. You can even cry out to Him. He will come. He will hold you close to His heart. For you are the beloved.

Dearest Lord Jesus, I cry out to You in my time of need, knowing You are my best friend. Thank You for rescuing me and restoring me. I trust in You alone. Amen.

Wondrous Joy

There were sheepherders camping in the neighborhood.
They had set night watches over their sheep. Suddenly, God's
angel stood among them and God's glory blazed around them.
They were terrified. The angel said, "Don't be afraid. I'm here
to announce a great and joyful event that is meant for every-
body, worldwide: A Savior has just been born in David's town,
a Savior who is Messiah and Master. This is what you're to
look for: a baby wrapped in a blanket and lying in a manger."
At once the angel was joined by a huge angelic choir singing
God's praises: Glory to God in the heavenly heights, peace to
all men and women on earth who please him.
LUKE 2:8–14 MSG

Spend a little time imagining that glorious night when Jesus was born. What indescribable joy. No human event can match it. No earthly proclamation can resonate with the soul like that single announcement. No song can be as beautiful as what the choir of angels sang on that starry night. No baby born has ever held such a gift for humankind.

May the joy of that holy night never be forgotten. May we never slip into ambivalence or skepticism or make Christmas into just another commercial holiday. May we ever remember the miracle of miracles that arrived on that not-so-silent night in Bethlehem.

Lord, I am in awe of the way You came to walk among us,
to save us, and to make us Your forever friends. Amen.

It Only Takes a Moment

For I am overwhelmed and desperate, and you alone know which way I ought to turn to miss the traps my enemies have set for me. (There's one—just over there to the right!) No one gives me a passing thought. No one will help me; no one cares a bit what happens to me. Then I prayed to Jehovah. "Lord," I pled, "you are my only place of refuge. Only you can keep me safe."
PSALM 142:3–5 TLB

We live in a fragile world, and people are fickle. That can be an unhappy mix, if not dangerous. How fast, for instance, can a fine and long-standing reputation be ruined in a moment of slanderous gossip? How easily can an amicable friendship twist into disdain from a misunderstood text? How speedily can a person be decimated emotionally with a few pieces of recklessly cruel comments and comebacks on social media?

Even though King David knew nothing of our modern times and technology, he knew everything about trials. We can read about his famous laments in Psalms. And yet there always came an answer—God.

Yes, it may only take a moment to be embroiled in trouble, but it also only takes a moment to pray.

Lord, please place Your mighty hand of protection on me, for this world is a dangerous place to be. Amen.

Hold Me Fast!

Who stood up for me against the wicked? Who took
my side against evil workers? If GOD hadn't been there
for me, I never would have made it. The minute I said,
"I'm slipping, I'm falling," your love, GOD, took hold
and held me fast. When I was upset and beside myself,
you calmed me down and cheered me up.
PSALM 94:16–19 MSG

You found a pretty little mountain to climb and off you go. But
as you hike along the winding switchbacks, the trail goes from
safe and gentle to narrow and rocky. A craggy bluff rises on one
side of you, while the other side plunges steeply. Had you taken
a wrong turn? Was the map inaccurate? Should you return? Then
the sky that had looked friendly turns menacing and pelts you
with mortar-like raindrops. With great speed you turn around to
head back, but the rocks beneath your feet give way and you
begin to slide.

Whether your slippery slope is on a real hillside or the peril
comes from another source, cling to God. Tell Him that you are
slipping and falling. The Lord promises to hold you fast. To calm
you and to cheer you. When life's trail becomes treacherous, and
the day turns into the darkest night, God is there.

Trust Him. He won't let you down.

Lord, please help me. I'm falling. Hold me fast! Amen.

Remembered Forever!

"Can a woman forget her nursing child, that she should have no compassion on the son of her womb? Even these may forget, yet I will not forget you. Behold, I have engraved you on the palms of my hands; your walls are continually before me."
ISAIAH 49:15–16 ESV

As you mill around your favorite antique store, you may be surprised to see old photographs of people that are up for sale. And you might wonder, *If those are family members, why are their pictures being sold to strangers?* Perhaps the photos had been passed down for so many generations that no one knows who they are anymore?

That isn't an easy thought to bear, that on this earthly plain we might be forgotten at some point. All our personal struggles and triumphs. The clever way Granddad proposed to Grandma. The distinguished military honors. The child's sweet nothings whispered at bedtime. No family members—no matter how sentimental—will be able to keep the memories of all the generations alive forever. But there is good news that washes over these sad thoughts like a refreshing spring rain. We can have the assurance that God remembers. God says, "Can a woman forget her nursing child? I will not forget you. I have engraved you on the palms of My hands." What a divine answer to a human heartbreak!

Oh, the joy of being remembered by God for all time.

Lord, I embrace this glorious truth! I love You too! Amen.

Bearing Much Fruit

*"I am the vine; you are the branches. If you remain
in me and I in you, you will bear much fruit;
apart from me you can do nothing."*
JOHN 15:5 NIV

Comparing ourselves to others is a real joy slayer. No matter how great our talents or noble our thoughts or beautiful our deeds, we will always find other people who appear to lead more illustrious and saintly lives. One of the ploys of the enemy is to get Christians so busy playing the comparison game that they become crippled with discouragement and inaction—essentially shoved into a corner, joyless and useless.

When we allow ourselves to be spiritually paralyzed in our deeds and talents, then we say to the Sovereign God, "You missed the mark when You made me." And we are basically refusing to acknowledge the supernatural power of God to change us, inspire us and others, and do what He promised—to have us bear much fruit.

So you still think your kind deeds are not wholly perfect? Do them anyway. You think your talents aren't so award-winning and stellar? Keep offering them up to God. Noble thoughts not quite there yet? Keep thinking honorable thoughts. The Lord is the Vine, and we are His branches. When we remain in Him, we can trust the Lord for the good fruit that is to come!

*Lord, I choose to find joy in the good work
You've given me until You take me home. Amen.*

The Seeds of Joy!

*He said to them, "Go into all the world
and preach the gospel to all creation."*
MARK 16:15 NIV

Some trees—like the maple—seem kind of magical in the way their helicopter-like seeds whirl to the ground. If these seeds get caught in a breeze, they will take flight, heading off to parts unknown. These whirlybirds are as endearingly cute as they are marvelous. God created such unique ways to spread His vegetation!

Like these merry winged seeds, we as Christians are to spread the joyful seeds of the Gospel far and wide. Even if you don't travel around the world as a missionary, you can be supportive in many ways. Maybe you could host an appreciation luncheon in your home or offer to mail care packages. Perhaps you could give a donation to ongoing mission work or volunteer to make up Christmas boxes for the kids they minister to.

Also, we can be the spreaders of good news in our local areas. We shouldn't be pushy or argumentative, but we should be winsome, simply telling folks where our joy springs from. Yes, to spread the seeds of the Gospel is to spread the seeds of joy!

*Lord, I want to share the Gospel. Give me the
right words to share with Your beloved. Amen.*

From the Soul

Whatever you do [whatever your task may be],
work from the soul [that is, put in your very best effort],
as [something done] for the Lord and not for men.
COLOSSIANS 3:23 AMP

All you have to do in your retirement is to tend a little garden. After having a high-powered executive job, tending a patch of dirt seems like a lowly calling. And yet your pastor encouraged you to make the most of it for the Lord—to see what happens when you work from the soul. So you did.

And that garden flourished with your loving attentions. Sometime later, a neighbor lady came over and decided to join you in your labors. You made a new friend, and with the combined efforts there was more than enough veggies not only to feed you both but to help a few people down the street who'd known hard times. Then the flowers bloomed so big, it was a shame not to share those too, so you took them to a local nursing home. People perked up, knowing that "flower Friday" was the day there would be fragrant blossoms on all the dining room tables.

Then one day, unexpectedly, you felt it—a warm smile coming down from heaven itself. You could almost hear the words aloud: "Well done." And in that moment, you couldn't remember ever having so much joy.

Lord, no matter what I do, may I
always work from the soul! Amen.

True Happiness

*Those who love money will never have enough. How
meaningless to think that wealth brings true happiness!*
ECCLESIASTES 5:10 NLT

Everyone is searching for happiness. Sometimes we choose
good things toward that goal, but the love of money has a way
of getting mixed up in the stew of life. And once a stew is made,
we tend to eat it.

We're discerning and savvy enough to know that money isn't
the ultimate joy, but we also wonder, *Why does it always seem
like those cautions about wealth are made by people who are
well-to-do?* The rich sure do look happy traveling at their leisure.
Eating and drinking the best of everything. Living a lavish lifestyle
simply because it suits them. So you think maybe you'd like to try
big money for a while to make your own conclusion!

Yes, God certainly gave you the free will to make that choice.
But remember that there's a little nugget of truth that goes with
that big nugget of gold. If you love money, you will never have
enough of it. The continual striving to get more cash and the strain
to never lose it can destroy one's joy and damage one's soul. Is
money evil? No. But making wealth into a god isn't pleasing to
the Lord. And as Christians, bringing delight to the Lord is the
only way to true happiness.

Lord, I love You above everyone and everything! Amen.

Know Them by Heart

Remember what Christ taught, and let his words enrich your lives and make you wise; teach them to each other and sing them out in psalms and hymns and spiritual songs, singing to the Lord with thankful hearts.
COLOSSIANS 3:16 TLB

When Jesus was tempted, He never got blindsided. He knew His scriptures, and He used them. We see that fact played out clearly in Matthew 4 when Jesus was tested in various ways in the wilderness. When the devil tempted Jesus while He was fasting, Jesus answered, "It is written: 'Man shall not live on bread alone, but on every word that comes from the mouth of God'" (Matthew 4:4 NIV).

So when the tempter comes to lead you astray or to harm you or steal your joy, answer him back with the truth of the scriptures. Let the words of the Bible enrich you and make you wise. Teach the scriptures to each other. Sing them out in psalms and hymns. Know them by heart.

Jesus did.

Father God, I admit I am not very good at memorizing things, let alone passages of scripture. Please give me not only the courage to live by Your truths, but the focus and discipline to commit them to memory. In Jesus' holy name I pray, amen.

Laughing at the Days to Come

She is clothed with strength and dignity; she can laugh at the days to come. She speaks with wisdom, and faithful instruction is on her tongue. She watches over the affairs of her household and does not eat the bread of idleness. Her children arise and call her blessed; her husband also, and he praises her: "Many women do noble things, but you surpass them all."

PROVERBS 31:25–29 NIV

Life is rascally hard. It can be like standing barefoot on a freshly stirred ant mound. Mmm-hmm. And so it goes with some of our earthly days.

But the Bible tells us that we are to laugh at the days to come. Oh? Even when we know that some of those days will be filled with troubles far worse than an ant sting? Wouldn't that just make us gullible or delusional or crazy? Or here's one other possibility. . .

It would make us trusting.

Does that mean with a little faith, God will let Christians live a trouble-free life here? No. But it does mean that when we trust the Lord for all things, He will escort us through this fallen world with love and compassion, mercy and grace. Then sometime later, the Lord will escort us into a place He's prepared for us—a place He calls heaven.

Lord, thank You that because my eternal future is secure, I can indeed laugh at the earthly days to come. Amen.

What a Promise!

Give generously to them and do so without a grudging heart;
then because of this the LORD your God will bless you in
all your work and in everything you put your hand to.
DEUTERONOMY 15:10 NIV

Sure, it's fun to wolf down a gooey slice of homemade birthday cake and then tear into a pile of gifts. Who doesn't want to be in the receiving line for those delights? But giving also has some joyful benefits. What about when you hand that homeless man a care package full of toiletries and fresh socks? That smile you put on his face was reflected on your face too. What about that special time of prayer for a loved one? Didn't you also feel an intimate closeness with the Lord? And the forgiveness you'd given someone who'd hurt your feelings. . .didn't that experience give your soul some newfound freedom?

The prayers we offer up for others, the forgiveness we extend, the donations we give of our time, talent, and money—all of it—don't merely change the benefactors of our many gifts. They change us too. Just as we help others, we too are forever altered. And beyond the growth we will encounter, the Lord also reminds us that if we give generously and without a grudging heart, He will bless us in our work. What a promise. What a joy!

Lord, show me how to give and how
to do it with merry gusto! Amen.

A Joyful Walk

Most of the crowd spread their cloaks on the road, and others cut branches from the trees and spread them on the road. And the crowds that went before him and that followed him were shouting, "Hosanna to the Son of David! Blessed is he who comes in the name of the Lord! Hosanna in the highest!" And when he entered Jerusalem, the whole city was stirred up, saying, "Who is this?"
MATTHEW 21:8–10 ESV

We are a capricious lot. One day we might praise a colleague, and then the next week we might engage in a bit of rumormongering about her. Perhaps it was something that was mentioned in confidence, yes, but the info didn't seem all that condemning. As it turned out though, that smallish statement about a past indiscretion ruined the woman's reputation and career. It destroyed more than one friendship, and the gossip grieved the Holy Spirit.

When Christ came to earth, humanity proved itself to be even more dangerously capricious. One day people were spreading their cloaks before Jesus and crying, "Hosanna in the highest!" and soon after, people were shouting, "Crucify Him!"

As Christians, may we pray for consistency in our faith. Even when the road is rough, we can experience a steady and joyful and peaceful walk with Christ.

Oh Lord, I confess that as a Christian I haven't always been consistent. Please forgive me and help my ways to be Your ways. Amen.

A Sense of Joyous Wonder

Blessed be the LORD, the God of Israel, who alone does wondrous things. Blessed be his glorious name forever; may the whole earth be filled with his glory! Amen and Amen!
PSALM 72:18–19 ESV

Kids are little mystical beings of wonder, aren't they? Their belly laughs are infectious in the most delightful ways. Their innocent questions boggle the mind. Their curiosity is unparalleled. Their sense of adventure leaves us breathless. When they stomp in a mud puddle, they are little Einsteins, experimenting with the dynamics of the splash. Or contemplating what happens when dirt mixes with water. And then what happens when that grimy concoction covers them from head to toe.

Even though childhood research can sometimes leave moms a little frazzled, it can also be amazing to watch. As adults we do tend to lose some of that sense of wonder. But as we mature, may we never forget that God is about wonder too. He has not only made a creation exploding with all things marvelous; God continues to do wonder-filled things throughout the earth and in our lives.

Creator God, I can barely contain my awe of You and Your mighty works. Your creation is majestic and well ordered yet unfathomable. I praise You and thank You. Blessed be Your glorious name forever! In Jesus' name I pray, amen.

Embrace the Joy!

*Don't fret or worry. Instead of worrying, pray. Let petitions
and praises shape your worries into prayers, letting God
know your concerns. Before you know it, a sense of God's
wholeness, everything coming together for good, will come
and settle you down. It's wonderful what happens when
Christ displaces worry at the center of your life.*

PHILIPPIANS 4:6–7 MSG

People are prone to fret. And well, there's a lot of stuff out there that seems worthy of our worry, right? You're stressed about your child's rebellious streak, your spouse's long hours at work, your lackluster job, the dust bunnies that never get vacuumed, your stepfather's cruel words, your lack of good sleep, your car's iffy stability, not to mention your own iffy stability!

How can we live with such turmoil and troubles? One faith step at a time. Pray like you mean it—like your supplications not only are being heard but will be answered. Trust in the Lord and His mercies. As it says beautifully in Philippians 4:6–7 (MSG), "Let petitions and praises shape your worries into prayers, letting God know your concerns. Before you know it, a sense of God's wholeness, everything coming together for good, will come and settle you down."

When we're not wringing our hands in worry, we can more easily embrace the joy that was meant for us.

*Lord, I want to trust in You fully. I am now
trading in my worry for Your joy! Amen.*

A Thing of Beauty

Slowness to anger makes for deep understanding;
a quick-tempered person stockpiles stupidity.
PROVERBS 14:29 MSG

This old world is chugging along, belching blue smoke—fueled by the worthless fumes of impatience—when what we really need is the clean-burning and grace-filled power of forbearance!

Don't you love it when people are patient with you? It brings such joy. Patience may not be displayed on a pedestal with bright and bold halogen lights, but it should be! Patience is a thing of beauty. Why? Because the Lord is patient with us even when we don't deserve it. How lovely. And He wants us to give this beautiful gift to others. For instance, when we come across a grumpy man behind the counter, we have no idea what that man is going through. He may have gout and with every movement his foot is riddled with pain. Or he may have lost his beloved wife of thirty years and every day he goes home desperately lonely. We just don't know. But God does. And the Lord will smile on you when you offer that gentleman a little mercy. May our patience always be on display for all to enjoy.

Mighty God, I confess that sometimes I have a quick
temper. And when I'm angry, my joy flies out the window.
I am going to trust You that together we can grow me up
into a woman of patience! In Jesus' name I pray, amen.

The Stones Will Cry Out

When he came near the place where the road goes down
the Mount of Olives, the whole crowd of disciples began
joyfully to praise God in loud voices for all the miracles
they had seen: "Blessed is the king who comes in the name
of the Lord!" "Peace in heaven and glory in the highest!"
Some of the Pharisees in the crowd said to Jesus,
"Teacher, rebuke your disciples!" "I tell you," he replied,
"if they keep quiet, the stones will cry out."
LUKE 19:37–40 NIV

The comedian offered his punch line, but he was met with a terrifying silence. No. One. Laughed. And there on that stage, that poor, dear man sort of died. The joke had been a good one, and it had been delivered with precision. What happened, then? Through no fault of his own, the comedian was simply playing to a hostile crowd.

As Christians, we are a little like that entertainer. We too are on stage with a good message—the best there is—but we're sometimes facing a hostile crowd. From the moment Christ offered His gift of salvation, much of humankind has been pridefully ignoring the need for a Savior. But we must speak up. We need to praise the Lord, to tell of His miracles, and to share the reason for our hope and joy. And if people try to quiet us, we must not remain quiet.

Lord, I praise You for all You've done.
My heart is overflowing with gratitude! Amen.

Such Good Medicine!

A joyful heart is good medicine,
but a crushed spirit dries up the bones.
PROVERBS 17:22 ESV

Some studies have shown that loneliness and depression can be harmful to your health. But you don't really need research data to remind you of that fact. Common sense tells you that those emotions wear on your body, mind, and spirit. So if a joyful heart is good medicine, how can it be found?

The greatest source of joy is God Himself, of course, but our Lord offers His people a plethora of joys. The wonders of creation. Friendships. Daily fellowshipping with Him. Good and meaningful work. Marriage. Culinary delights. Learning and exploring. Sporting events. Praising God with other believers in Christ. The blessings of children. This list really could go on and on.

Because of sin in our fallen world, there are also plenty of not-so-good things around that will crush your spirit—such as stress from worry, friendships peppered with strife, too much social media and news, addictions of any kind, or rebellion against biblical principles. This list can go on and on too.

We have a choice: a heart that gathers miseries or a heart that gathers merry.

Dear Jesus, show me how to have a merry heart.
I need less gloom and more gladness. Amen.

Love Each Other

"My command is this: Love each
other as I have loved you."
JOHN 15:12 NIV

We all have those special people in our lives that bring us joy. Big smiles. Merry laughter. Good feelings down to our toes. You know just who they are. You see them coming and your arms automatically get ready to hug. They make your world a happier place to be. You surely must love them dearly. Have you told them? There is no better time than the present to tell your loved ones that you care.

Just imagine sitting at the funeral of your beloved, and you'd never said what was on your heart, what really mattered. The time for sending bouquets of flowers is now. The time for heart sharing is now. The time for saying, "I love you!" is now.

Who is on that list? How about adding God? He would certainly appreciate being at the top of that love list.

Father God, I haven't told You lately how much I love
You, and I want to do that right now. I love You! Thank You
for all the wonderful people You've placed in my heart.
And thank You for Your divine gifts of love, peace, mercy,
and grace. These gifts have helped me to grow into
a woman of joy. In Jesus' name I pray, amen.

When I See You Again

"When a woman gives birth, she has a hard time, there's no getting around it. But when the baby is born, there is joy in the birth. This new life in the world wipes out memory of the pain. The sadness you have right now is similar to that pain, but the coming joy is also similar. When I see you again, you'll be full of joy, and it will be a joy no one can rob from you. You'll no longer be so full of questions."
JOHN 16:21–23 MSG

Jesus says to His beloved, "When I see you again, you'll be full of joy, and it will be a joy no one can rob from you." Those should be some of the most comforting words ever said.

On impossible days when you are bone tired. When you wonder what God is up to. When you wonder a thousand things that seem to have few answers, well, the Bible gives us hope that surpasses all hope. Jesus says to His followers, "When I see you again."

Embrace that glorious promise of God. It's real, and it's not just offered to a world in need—but it's offered to each of us personally.

Lord God Almighty, thank You for salvation in Christ and that I am a new creature. Thank You for Your many blessings, including the gift of joy. In Jesus' name I pray, amen.

Out of the Shadows

"The LORD himself goes before you and will be with
you; he will never leave you nor forsake you.
Do not be afraid; do not be discouraged."
DEUTERONOMY 31:8 NIV

You don't really know what's wrong. You have good reason to be happy, but you wake up depressed. Other people around you seem to have joy. Your family, your social media buddies, your Bible study gals, and even the ladies in your car pool—they all seem to be as happy as well-fed clams! Then there is you. You'd like to rise up and protest, but you just feel too downtrodden to bother.

Sometimes people encounter occasional seasons of depression, and sometimes they have no idea what causes it. The bottom line is, if you need help, get it. If you need to talk to someone, don't be embarrassed to find some good Christian counseling. Life is not easy.

But do remember, as you go through the shadows of life, God is still there. Do not be afraid. Do not be discouraged. God will not leave you or forsake you. He'll walk with you through the shadows of life and bring you out into the sun once again. Take His hand.

Lord, I don't know why I'm so down, but I thank You
for Your everlasting love, for Your infinite patience,
and for the joy that I know will come again. Amen.

Locating That Smile Again

*"Take my yoke upon you, and learn from me, for I am gentle
and lowly in heart, and you will find rest for your souls.
For my yoke is easy, and my burden is light."*
MATTHEW 11:29–30 ESV

Have you ever tried to open a newly purchased gadget from the store but the goofy thing came ultrasealed in one of those heavy-duty, plastic jobbers? The container is sturdy enough to be used for a time capsule! As you try to rip, snip, and bust your way in, you work yourself into a tizzy. Then suddenly, you see an easy-open tab. Good grief.

Sometimes that's the way we live our lives. We assume from watching the world that we are to live in that full-blown tizzy mode. Yes, life is indeed hard. But Christ says, "Take my yoke upon you, and learn from me, for I am gentle and lowly in heart, and you will find rest for your souls. For my yoke is easy, and my burden is light."

Read those verses every morning if you need to. Write them on a sticky note for your mirror, fridge, or forehead if necessary! They are words to get you through the day, to relax your shoulders along with your soul, and they are words to help you locate your smile again.

*Oh Lord, I keep trying to do life the hard way
without You. Show me how to do life Your way. Amen.*

O Taste!

O taste and see that the LORD is good;
happy are those who take refuge in him.
PSALM 34:8 NRSV

It seems you've been making coffee with that preground canned stuff for as long as the sun has been rising. You drink it down to the dregs and tell yourself, "Not bad." You've heard there's a better brew out there, but you find yourself just making do. Then a gal friend says, "No more of that cheap and tasteless brown water for you. I'm taking you out for a real cup of coffee. No arguments. I'm buying!"

You could say no out of habit or out of your usual skepticism, but there's something about that twinkle in her eye that makes you go. So you sit down with her in one of those gourmet coffeehouses, take a tentative taste of your beverage—oh, and slurp off that cool, heart-shaped foam—then you take a few more serious sips.

You sigh and run the gamut of emotions—one being anger at yourself for staying in such a needless rut, and another being that you're grateful there's so much more beyond your tin-can world.

In our earthly lives, may we never make do with what the world and the enemy have to offer us. May we remember the words, "O taste and see that the LORD is good." You will never want to go back.

Lord, I have tasted Your goodness,
and I am filled with joy! Amen.

Face-to-Face with God!

*In the same way, we can see and understand only a little
about God now, as if we were peering at his reflection
in a poor mirror; but someday we are going to see him
in his completeness, face-to-face. Now all that I know is
hazy and blurred, but then I will see everything clearly,
just as clearly as God sees into my heart right now.*

1 CORINTHIANS 13:12 TLB

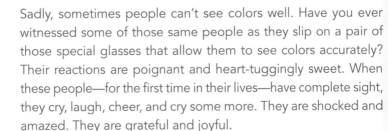

Sadly, sometimes people can't see colors well. Have you ever witnessed some of those same people as they slip on a pair of those special glasses that allow them to see colors accurately? Their reactions are poignant and heart-tuggingly sweet. When these people—for the first time in their lives—have complete sight, they cry, laugh, cheer, and cry some more. They are shocked and amazed. They are grateful and joyful.

And so it goes with our limited view of God on earth. But that partial soul sight we experience is only temporary. As Christians, someday we will be in heaven, and we will see our Lord in His completeness—face-to-face. Oh, here's to those beautiful, glorious days—the homegoing of all believers. Such complete joy!

---

*Lord, I am looking forward to one day seeing You face-to-face!
Thank You for this promise and hope. Amen.*

Welcome Signs

Anyone you forgive, I also forgive. And what I have forgiven—
if there was anything to forgive—I have forgiven in the
sight of Christ for your sake, in order that Satan might not
outwit us. For we are not unaware of his schemes.
2 CORINTHIANS 2:10–11 NIV

When you've invited a dear friend over for lunch, you thrill at the sound of the bell, you throw open the door, and you give your beloved friend a welcoming hug. That is how we react to friends. But Satan is the enemy of one's soul. We never want to offer him any kind of open door in our lives. And yet, that's what we do when we stubbornly refuse to forgive someone. Or when we flirt with a fleeting temptation. Or when we dabble in pride, even if it comes from an outwardly innocuous place. Or when we allow ourselves to forget how truly vital it is to stay in close communion with our Lord. Be aware that Satan can use the most seemingly innocent and unexpected things in our lives to drive a wedge between us and God.

May we stay ever near to Christ so the enemy will never see a welcome sign on our souls.

Lord, help me to always know the ploys of Satan,
and help me to flee from him. Amen.

I Have Called You Friends!

"No longer do I call you servants, for the servant does not know what his master is doing; but I have called you friends, for all that I have heard from my Father I have made known to you."
JOHN 15:15 ESV

The book of John reminds us that Jesus calls us His friends. What can we do with such a remarkable blessing? How do we live and talk to God in the light of this astounding revelation?

Well, perhaps you see the sun burst through a dark storm cloud and you tell God of your awe. If you see tensions finally ease in a stressful work environment, thank Him. A friend calls to give you a word of support. Tell the Lord how that encourages you. Maybe you're frazzled from too much work and not enough sleep, and so you have a little meltdown. Tell the Lord about it. He's listening and He wants to help. When your child hugs your neck and gives you a big smoochy kiss, well, send a smile up to the heavens.

So talking to Jesus is sort of like a running conversation on and off all day? It's like talking to the dearest friend you could ever imagine, only better? It's not a tedious ritual but an intimate relationship? A joyful yes to all!

Jesus, I choose to live my life completely connected to You. You bring me joy that is unsurpassed. Amen.

Get Some Rest

*Then, because so many people were coming and going
that they did not even have a chance to eat, he said to
them, "Come with me by yourselves to a
quiet place and get some rest."*
MARK 6:31 NIV

The little girl was in bad need of a nap. She was so tired she'd been reduced to a mess of sweaty curls and a pair of wailing lungs. The little girl tried to fight it though, and so instead of placing her head on the pillow, she defiantly tried to play with her stuffed animal. She fussed and talked and whimpered. Then in utter exhaustion, the little darling finally stopping fighting what she needed and drifted off into dreamland. Good satisfying sleep. It was what she needed to be refreshed so she could go back to her skipping, exploring, laughing, learning, coloring, and baking cookies with her mom. She just needed that rest.

Are we fighting what we need—rest? Working nonstop, even on Sunday? Fussing when we should be drifting? If we let ourselves get too exhausted, life will not go well for us. We won't be able to work, to play, to enjoy life. Even Jesus said, "Come with me by yourselves to a quiet place and get some rest."

*Holy Spirit, I admit I'm a workaholic at times.
Please teach me how to rest. Amen.*

The Hope of Spring

For we know that the whole creation has been groaning together in the pains of childbirth until now. And not only the creation, but we ourselves, who have the firstfruits of the Spirit, groan inwardly as we wait eagerly for adoption as sons, the redemption of our bodies. For in this hope we were saved. Now hope that is seen is not hope. For who hopes for what he sees? But if we hope for what we do not see, we wait for it with patience.

ROMANS 8:22–25 ESV

The wind blew hard, slapping you in the face like an icy towel. March had turned quite ugly, with temps that made you never want to leave the house again. You rush inside and stand at the window, rubbing your arms. That stand of old, barren elms looks more like a graveyard of trees than anything with promising, flourishing potential. In fact, it's almost impossible to imagine them full of green, budding life. But even in the cold dusk, there at the window, you hold on to hope and wait with patience for the spring that you know will come.

As Christians, we have the promise of being adopted as God's children, the hope of heaven, and the redemption of our bodies. Yes, we wait with patience for the beauty of what is to come for those who love Christ!

Lord, I am filled up to the brim with hope
as I await the joys of heaven. Amen.

Bumbly but Beautiful

Jesus told this simple story, but they had no idea what he was talking about. So he tried again. "I'll be explicit, then. I am the Gate for the sheep. All those others are up to no good—sheep stealers, every one of them. But the sheep didn't listen to them. I am the Gate. Anyone who goes through me will be cared for—will freely go in and out, and find pasture. A thief is only there to steal and kill and destroy. I came so they can have real and eternal life, more and better life than they ever dreamed of."
JOHN 10:6–10 MSG

It's hard not to like sheep. They're so fluffy and endearing. Granted, they have a perpetual case of the munchies, but they make such beseeching supplications. Baaaaaaa! What's not to love? But sheep are also bumbly, and they have been known to get themselves into trouble. Jesus likes to call us His sheep, and He has good reason to. We humans have been known to get ourselves into trouble too.

We face peril every time we forget that Jesus isn't just a gate to go through—Jesus is THE gate. Everyone who goes through the Lord's gate will be well cared for and will find real and eternal life.

Lord, my Shepherd, when I am tempted to try another path or gate, please guide me to the way I should go! Amen.

Oh, the Many Joys!

*Now there was leaning on Jesus' bosom
one of His disciples, whom Jesus loved.*
JOHN 13:23 NKJV

When you read John 13:23, and reread it, you get the clear impression we're not talking about a distant deity. This scripture—like so many others in the Bible—reveals an invitation to encounter a closeness with our Lord. You don't generally lean on someone or allow someone to lean on you unless you both trust each other fully, find joy in each other's company, and love each other without reservation. So beautiful, isn't it?

But when we think of religion—sometimes even Christianity—we may conjure up words like *stodgy, passionless, archaic, empty rituals, works, rejection, critical, rules,* and *lifeless.* Oh dear. No wonder the world wants to run the other way!

But that's not what Jesus is about. When the Lord came to us, He brought words and phrases like *refreshment, beauty, lavish love, healing touches, divine intimacy, quiet waters, dramatic rescues, sacrifice, restoration, imperishability, grace, openheartedness, glorious declarations, supernatural wonders, brilliance, singing, miracles, vanquishing the enemy, freedom from evil, rebirth, an invitation to heaven, timelessness, happiness,* and *flourish!*

May we all embrace the sweet salvation and the many joys that Christ has to offer!

Oh Lord, I am in awe of who You really are! Amen.

Satisfying All Around

*Everyone enjoys giving good advice, and how wonderful
it is to be able to say the right thing at the right time!*
PROVERBS 15:23 TLB

In an effort to sleep better, you make the bedroom as dark as you can. Perfect. At 2 a.m. though, you wake up to go to the bathroom. How predictable. You tiptoe, trying not to wake your husband. Can do. You're sensing your way through a pitch-black space—better than a bat—when you hear a wham. Which would be the sound of your forehead crashing into a wall hanging. You holler. All the lights snap on. Game over. Good sleep? Forget about it. If only there had been a bit more light. . .

In our Christian walk, good and godly advice can be a little like that extra light to help us on our way—to keep us from stumbling around in the dark. People enjoy giving away good advice too. Ahhh, yes, just the right words at the right time. Pleasant. Valuable. Satisfying all around.

May we pray to be the givers of wise advice as well as recipients of the same gift.

*Dear God, please lead me to people who have wisdom
when giving advice, and may I always have the right words
when I speak to others. In Jesus' name I pray, amen.*

Our Sweaty Little Grip

Casting all your cares [all your anxieties, all your worries, and all your concerns, once and for all] on Him, for He cares about you [with deepest affection, and watches over you very carefully].

1 PETER 5:7 AMP

You know that as a Christian you are to give all your troubles to the Lord. Got that one down, right? Well, sort of. But when you try to sleep at night, you can sense there is still that one "thing" that keeps bugging you. That last niggling worry is like a kite that is meant to fly away out of your control and into God's domain. So in a moment of profound trust in the Lord—since that is what's required—you pry your fingers off the kite and set it free from your sweaty little grip. It takes off, but it sputters. You may have to keep trying, but at some point the winged toy does indeed take off into the sweet breezes of heaven. And as you let out the string more and more and more, your heart soars as it was meant to soar. God has this.

What is the one "thing" that is keeping you from letting go and embracing joy?

Jesus, may I always cast all of my cares on You, even the ones I want to cling to! Amen.

Going All Out

"There are many homes up there where my Father lives, and I am going to prepare them for your coming. When everything is ready, then I will come and get you, so that you can always be with me where I am. If this weren't so, I would tell you plainly."
JOHN 14:2–3 TLB

It's only September, but in your heart you know Christmas is coming soon. You're so excited. When no one is paying attention, you start playing holiday music, and you even hum the carols while driving here and there. You just can't help yourself. You love everything about Christmas. The beautiful ornaments and lights. The festivities and the glow on everyone's face and in everyone's heart. You even find joy in the velvet antlers on your husband's head and the eggnog mustache on your upper lip! This year you have decided that you're going all out. The most delicious food for your holiday feast. Decor with the most wow factor. The most profound music to lift the soul. Gifts to bring a hearty laugh. The best of everything for your family. Nothing is too good for your beloved.

When Christ was here, He said He was going to prepare a place for us. He intends to go all out. Nothing will be too good for His beloved family.

Lord Jesus, I love being part of Your family, and I'm excited about this wonderful place You've prepared for me. Amen.

Joy Comes Back to Us

Rejoice with those who rejoice,
weep with those who weep.
ROMANS 12:15 ESV

The woman sat alone in her lush high-rise apartment with her head in her palms. She needed to cry, but something kept her dry-eyed. Through her fog of loneliness and pain, she wondered if she could hire someone as a professional weeper—someone to come alongside her and weep with her in times of crisis or sorrow. She had no idea, but it seemed reasonable, since people could hire anyone to do anything these days. And she certainly had the money to pay someone to be a friend. Then again, she had lots of friends, but no one seemed to have the time to listen—really listen—anymore, let alone cry with you when you were in need. Wasn't there a scripture about that somewhere in the Bible? She wasn't sure. But the woman was sure of one thing—society was much more eager to share in her good times than share in her burden.

As Christians, may we remember that joy comes from giving of one's time, one's heart, and even one's tears.

Lord God, may I never be so busy that I don't have
time to come alongside a friend who is suffering.
May I have a listening ear and a servant's heart
that I might hear. In Jesus' name I pray, amen.

More Fragile Than Glass

But he said to me, "My grace is sufficient for you, for my power is made perfect in weakness." Therefore I will boast all the more gladly of my weaknesses, so that the power of Christ may rest upon me.

2 CORINTHIANS 12:9 ESV

We have seen people speaking with tremendous confidence—celebrities, news anchors, and some of the positive-thinking gurus. They appear to have their lives together in every way. You know, their belief system. Their hair. Their personal lives. And yet, many times when we witness the rest of the story, we see that they are fragile in their breakability, in their follies and frailties, in their reckless behaviors and night terrors, and in their desperate need for a Savior—just like every other person on the face of the earth.

So what can we glean from this knowledge? We should give up the worthless pretense that we have it all together—that we are the masters of our little universes. We're not even the masters of our big toes to keep them from getting stubbed in the darkness!

We are beloved and fallen creations who need a daily dose of grace from the true Master of the universe. We must ever humble ourselves and welcome the paradox at every turn—that in our weakness, Christ's power is made perfect. He is sufficient!

Lord Jesus, I admit freely that I am weak and that Your grace is all I need! Amen.

I See Miracles

"Behold, I am the LORD, the God of all flesh.
Is anything too hard for me?"
JEREMIAH 32:27 ESV

We get up and go to work. We come home and eat. We go to bed. The next weekday, we repeat. Do this long enough without the Lord's input, and one may succumb to seeing life as a box filled with nothing more than what is dull and ordinary. We start thinking in terms of routine, mundane, safe, bland, and familiar. We can eventually become so desensitized by the world's pragmatisms and cynicisms, we might miss the marvels throughout creation, the mysteries being unveiled, and the miracles that are right before us.

Many people do take note of what they perceive as profound miracles—such as a paralyzed woman suddenly being able to walk. But what about all the other many wonders? Like the forgiveness between old friends? The fireworks of the night sky that remind us how small we are, but how big God is? The joyful birth of a child when that same mother had been assured of infertility? A couple reconciling and renewing their vows? The gallant burst of tulips through a coverlet of snow? The Holy Spirit's illumination of scripture? The beautiful words of encouragement to the brokenhearted? One more soul turning toward Christ?

Remember, every day is a supernatural walk in God's world. May we keep our spirits tuned in to what is really there.

Lord, my soul finds joy in Your daily miracles! Amen.

Who Am I?

*Therefore, if anyone is in Christ, the new creation
has come: The old has gone, the new is here!*
2 CORINTHIANS 5:17 NIV

Have you ever heard someone sing who clearly had no talent for it? Maybe you know her from church. The poor woman wanted to share her gift, so she belted out a song like she was performing on stage at a grand concert hall. But the musical sounds coming out of her mouth made people cringe and dogs howl—they even made the celestial lights flicker a bit.

You see, many of her family members were singers, so the woman felt some friendly coercion to follow in the same path. Hopefully, she'll discover that God made her special and with purpose, but it might not be in the area of music.

This conundrum happens every time we feel the pressure to put on the goals and dreams and talents of other people. As Christians we are a new creation, but when it comes to how that new creation should live—ask God. He'll guide you in the way you should go.

Yes, go to the Source of all life. Go to the One who made you to be wonderful—as you.

---

*Dearest Lord, I need Your guidance in the
way I should go with my life. I want to be the
woman of joy You created me to be! Amen.*

God's Path to Joy

*They have no sense of shame. They live for lustful pleasure
and eagerly practice every kind of impurity. But that isn't
what you learned about Christ. Since you have heard about
Jesus and have learned the truth that comes from him, throw
off your old sinful nature and your former way of life, which
is corrupted by lust and deception. Instead, let the Spirit
renew your thoughts and attitudes. Put on your new nature,
created to be like God—truly righteous and holy.*

EPHESIANS 4:19–24 NLT

While shopping with your darling little boy, he grabs what he thinks
is a toy off the shelf, stamps his foot, and hollers, "I want that toy!"
The item isn't a toy at all, but a sharp tool at the hardware store.

Even as Christians, don't we sometimes stamp our little feet
at God and demand a toy we think we want, even if it's not
what we should have? Yes, God wants His people to be happy,
but we should never beg for Him to approve of our sinful lifestyles—lifestyles that might seem fun and free at the time but will
do us great harm in the end. May we desire real happiness, the
kind that can only come from God.

---

*Holy Spirit, renew my thoughts and attitudes. Help me to put
on my new nature so that I can be righteous and holy. I know in
pleasing You I will come to know real and lasting joy. Amen.*

Do Not Be Afraid

Elisha answered, "Do not be afraid, for those who are with us are more than those who are with them." Then Elisha prayed and said, "LORD, please, open his eyes that he may see." And the LORD opened the servants eyes and he saw; and behold, the mountain was full of horses and chariots of fire surrounding Elisha.

2 KINGS 6:16–17 AMP

The night is dark. The coming day seems impossible. You trust the Lord as best you can, but you can't imagine how the Almighty is going to rescue you from the mess you've found yourself in. You have been misunderstood and your name has been ruined. You have nowhere to turn, and it feels as though all your friends have abandoned you. It will take a miracle. Nothing less. You pray. Then you back away to watch.

When your life feels hopeless and the road ahead impassable, these verses in 2 Kings become vital to meditate on. As followers of Christ there is power in our prayers. Know that if you could see beyond the veil into the spiritual realm, you would be able to see all the supernatural wonders that are carried out on your behalf!

Oh Lord, when I become afraid, help me to remember to pray and that You are a God with supernatural power. You are in control! Amen.

To Be Loved So Much

See what great love the Father has lavished on us, that we should be called children of God! And that is what we are! The reason the world does not know us is that it did not know him.

1 JOHN 3:1 NIV

The toddler rested on her mother's bosom, and with her tiny fingers she pulled her mother's gaze over to her. The warm and adoring look on the child's face as she gazed up into her mother's eyes could have melted a glacier. And the returned look of delight on the mother's face was pure enchantment. The mother then softly dotted kisses on her baby's face. It was obvious that the mom's heart had been happily stolen and that she had no need to ever get it back. Such joy—to love so much.

Since God is the author of love, He cares for you even more than the mother loves her child in this story. The Lord wants to call you His daughter—His own. How have you responded to this divine gift?

Almighty God, I thank You for loving me so lavishly that You sent Your only Son, Jesus, to die for me. I know that through Christ's death and resurrection I have been offered the gift of salvation for the forgiveness of sins. I accept this amazing love gift. Thank You for forgiving me and for giving me eternal life. I love You, Lord! In Jesus' holy name I pray, amen.

Gracious Speech

Let your speech always be gracious, seasoned with salt,
so that you may know how you ought to answer each person.
Colossians 4:6 esv

You're at work and you see your superior barreling down the hall-way in your general direction. Your coworkers have been known to murmur the word *battle-ax* as she passes by. *You* would never be guilty of saying that, of course! But it had been said of her. Why? Because her speech is anything but gracious. She berates and hollers. She slams her fist on the table. But this time when that formidable form marches down the hall, instead of slinking away into the bowels of the break room as usual, you smile and greet her warmly.

After your boss gives you a savage, narrow-eyed gawk, something seeps into her perpetual frown. What is it? A smile? Yes!

The Bible offers us guidance on how to live our lives, and this advice also covers our speech. We are to be gracious, even in the midst of grumpy. Hard to do, yes, but with some help from the Holy Spirit, we can indeed help to sweeten our workplace, our home, and our world.

Holy Spirit, I often run into people who are anxious and
irritable and anything but joyful. Please give me the
strength to respond to these people with graciousness.
Make me an instrument of Your peace. Amen.

Good Reason for Joy

*"Are not five sparrows sold for two copper coins? Yet not one
of them has [ever] been forgotten in the presence of God.
Indeed the very hairs of your head are all numbered. Do not
be afraid; you are far more valuable than many sparrows."*
LUKE 12:6–7 AMP

Your little boy finally settles down into the barber's chair for his very first haircut. What a day! He's in a booster seat, of course, so he can feel like a big boy. When the first snips happen, here and there, curly locks tumble to the floor. In spite of some trepidation, your boy tilts his chin high, trying to be brave. He looks so grown-up, a tear slips down your cheek as you start taking photos. It is one of those "firsts" after all! When the big event is over, you take him out for his favorite ice cream. What can you say? He is the apple of your eye.

And so it goes with you and God. He not only knows and cares about your first haircut; He numbers the hairs on your head. Imagine! No mother or father can boast of such extraordinary attention to detail. Or such tender concern or affectionate care. Think about it. Smile about it.

We have good reason for joy.

*Lord, thank You for loving me so much that
You know every little thing about me! Amen.*

Lost in the Minutiae

"'Love the Lord your God with all your heart and with all your soul and with all your mind and with all your strength.' The second is this: 'Love your neighbor as yourself.' There is no commandment greater than these."
MARK 12:30–31 NIV

Jillian frantically took so many photos of the sunset, she forgot to truly "see" the beauty before her. She left no time to allow her spirit to unwind in the spectacular fanfare and farewell of the day, nor in her hurry did she remember to thank the One who'd created it.

In our walk with Christ, how many times do we get so caught up in striving that we get swallowed up in the minutiae of life? We then complicate our existence unnecessarily and weaken our relationship with Christ.

Perhaps we need to step back and once again acknowledge the essentials of our faith. Now is always a good time to make those adjustments. The verses provided from Mark 12 are an excellent example of getting back to the basics. Yes, we need the whole of the Bible to live by, and yet if we love our Lord with all our heart and we love our neighbors as ourselves, would we not discover a truly wonderful Christian life? One of truth and beauty and joy?

Lord, help me not to get lost in the minutiae but stay focused on You all through the day. Amen.

An Open Heart

"See my hands and my feet, that it is I myself. Touch me,
and see. For a spirit does not have flesh and bones
as you see that I have." And when he had said this,
he showed them his hands and his feet.
Luke 24:39–40 esv

Make a tight fist. What happens? Your fingers get blotchy and pain filled. Some people actually live their lives with their spirits sort of tight knuckled like that. They become cynical and tough, inaccessible and narrow, not to mention itching for an argument. But living with a big Closed sign on your heart will only end in pain.

Even if the prospect of openness feels risky and scary, we must learn how to unfold our hands and free our hearts. We will be able to hug, to give, to help, to share, and to receive God's good gifts. The Lord will always be the finest example of having a generous heart with His beloved. So profoundly so, out of love Christ offered His open palms and His very life to humankind. He was then pierced on those same precious palms for our sakes on the cross. Jesus gave it all so that we could receive it all—the joy of life eternal.

Lord, even though it may not be easy at times, I want
to live my life as You did, with an openness to give and
receive. Thank You for Your beautiful example to us. Amen.

Cool Wind on a Hot Day

*"So repent [change your inner self—your old way of
thinking, regret past sins] and return [to God—seek
His purpose for your life], so that your sins may be
wiped away [blotted out, completely erased], so that
times of refreshing may come from the presence of
the Lord [restoring you like a cool wind on a hot day]."*

ACTS 3:19 AMP

Just before dinnertime—and when no one was looking—the little
boy scurried from the kitchen with a small bag of chips. He knew
his mom would soon ask him to come to supper, so he hid in his
closet and gobbled up the salty treats as quickly as he could. But
no matter how tasty, the boy realized that eating the chips in a
hurry wasn't really fun, especially since he knew that the smile on
his mom's face would soon vanish like the chips.

But the little boy was wise enough to know what to do next.
He ran to his mom, climbed up on her lap, and told her everything. He'd rather take the loving punishment than hide away with
what was going to ruin his supper as well as ruin the closeness
with his mom.

Confession feels good to the soul—like a cool wind on a
hot day.

*Lord, I admit I have done wrong, and I am truly sorry.
Please forgive me and help me to do better in the
future. I want to make You proud! Amen.*

Prepare Yourself

Put on the full armor of God [for His precepts are like the splendid armor of a heavily-armed soldier], so that you may be able to [successfully] stand up against all the schemes and the strategies and the deceits of the devil.

<small>EPHESIANS 6:11 AMP</small>

So you've stayed in close fellowship with the Lord, and now you see signs of spiritual growth. *And* your life is joy filled in many ways. Excellent. But do remember that the devil—the enemy of your soul—wants nothing of it. He comes to lie, to steal, and to destroy. When you become intimate with God, buckle your spiritual safety belt and keep an eye out for the schemes of the devil. They may come in many forms. Some of them may be bold and some of them might be sly and even light bearing. Those demonic whispers may include something akin to what Job's wife said to him when he was in the throes of calamity. Job 2:9 (TLB) reads, "His wife said to him, 'Are you still trying to be godly when God has done all this to you? Curse him and die.'"

What are some of the attacks you've experienced from the enemy? How have you and the Lord handled them?

Almighty God, please protect me from the many schemes of the devil. Help me to know Your Word and use it to stand firm against the enemy's attacks. In Jesus' powerful name I pray, amen.

This Joyous Jubilee

Let the heavens rejoice, let the earth be glad; let the sea resound, and all that is in it. Let the fields be jubilant, and everything in them; let all the trees of the forest sing for joy.
PSALM 96:11–12 NIV

Have you ever tapped your foot to a really great beat? Do you ever hum along with a tune that captures your heart? Maybe it makes you want to burst into song or dance a little.

There is a kind of music out there—in the heavens and earth—that seems to praise our creator God. The whistling zephyrs through the piney woods. The silvery, crisp birdsong in the meadow. The sea's thundering waves against the craggy cliffs. You could call it nature's jubilee of joy.

But beyond what we can hear, the Bible speaks poetically of nature making its tributes and praises to God, who is the Maker of all. Psalm 148:7–9 (ESV) says, "Praise the LORD from the earth, you great sea creatures and all deeps, fire and hail, snow and mist, stormy wind fulfilling his word! Mountains and all hills, fruit trees and all cedars!" How glorious!

Lord, I want to be a part of this joyous jubilee! I want to wake up in the morning with a song in my heart. I want to celebrate and honor You with all my being! Amen.

Over the Moon

*Light in a messenger's eyes brings joy to the heart,
and good news gives health to the bones.*
PROVERBS 15:30 NIV

The doctor arrives in the room and she gives you the official yes that you'd been waiting years for. The pregnancy test is positive, and your heart soars! Within seconds of leaving the office you're already planning your nest. The overall color scheme and decor of the nursery. The little booties, the outfits, the stuffed animals. The college fund account. Never too early, right? It's obvious you are over the moon with excitement concerning the news. Yes, the light in the doctor's eyes brought you such a surge of joy.

Messengers can bring many kinds of wonderful and welcome news. Such as your supervisor telling you that you got that promotion you'd hoped for. Or perhaps a clean blood test that shows no signs of a previous illness. Or maybe an anonymous gift of money to help you pay off your utility bill.

Do you know anyone who could use a message of joy today? An encouraging word of hope? A promise of good things to come?

---

*Holy Spirit, enlighten me today concerning who might
need my assistance. Show me the people I can touch
with good news or a kind deed. Let me be a messenger
who brings joy to someone's heart! Amen.*

Awaken!

Don't waste your time on useless work, mere busywork,
the barren pursuits of darkness. Expose these things for
the sham they are. It's a scandal when people waste their
lives on things they must do in the darkness where no one
will see. Rip the cover off those frauds and see how attractive
they look in the light of Christ. Wake up from your sleep,
climb out of your coffins; Christ will show you the light! So
watch your step. Use your head. Make the most of every
chance you get. These are desperate times!
EPHESIANS 5:11–16 MSG

In your wanderings, you come across a sleeping fawn in the woods. You know not to touch, and yet in that whisper hush, you draw closer. The fawn stays so still you worry that it's dead. But in a flash, you hear the snort of the mother. Suddenly, the tiny deer rouses and races off to be with its mum. You're left in awe of this sacred-like moment. You've been in the wild, and you've witnessed the awakening of a blessed creature.

How do we look when the world finds us—lifeless? Do people wonder if we've abandoned our faith?

May we sense the nudge of the Holy Spirit, awaken from our busywork, and run back into the light of Christ. May the world witness a sacred moment—our reawakening to life, to joy!

Lord, if I have been asleep in my faith, awaken
me with Your bright and beautiful light! Amen.

Giving Voice to the Word

Ascribe to the LORD, O heavenly beings, ascribe to the LORD glory and strength. Ascribe to the LORD the glory due his name; worship the LORD in the splendor of holiness. The voice of the LORD is over the waters; the God of glory thunders, the LORD, over many waters. The voice of the LORD is powerful; the voice of the LORD is full of majesty. The voice of the LORD breaks the cedars; the LORD breaks the cedars of Lebanon. He makes Lebanon to skip like a calf, and Sirion like a young wild ox. The voice of the LORD flashes forth flames of fire. The voice of the LORD shakes the wilderness; the LORD shakes the wilderness of Kadesh. The voice of the LORD makes the deer give birth and strips the forests bare, and in his temple all cry, "Glory!"

PSALM 29:1–9 ESV

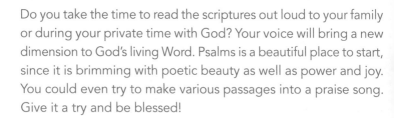

Do you take the time to read the scriptures out loud to your family or during your private time with God? Your voice will bring a new dimension to God's living Word. Psalms is a beautiful place to start, since it is brimming with poetic beauty as well as power and joy. You could even try to make various passages into a praise song. Give it a try and be blessed!

Lord, I love reading, memorizing, and speaking Your Word. Illuminate my heart as I glorify You. Amen.

Joy in Mercy

*"Shouldn't you have had mercy on your
fellow servant just as I had on you?"*
MATTHEW 18:33 NIV

You've about had it. Your whole body feels like a pressure cooker that's about to blow. That uncle of yours is snorting and laughing at your expense. He's disrespectful—and being a grown man, he should know better, right? You feel a trickle of hatred seeping in and your joy fleeing. You want your joy back, but the two sentiments cannot coexist.

You're in a social pickle, not to mention a spiritual predicament. You want to lash out at your uncle. You want to shame him into repentance. Tell him how hurt you are. You want to withhold your love from him. Or spit in his coffee! Well, maybe not that last one.

At some point though, you know you're going to have to face Matthew 18:33. Ask God to remind you of some of the times in which you jeered at other folks or when you were rude. Miraculously, some past incidences may soon arrive out of your memory banks. You will see once again how merciful God is to you when you falter or fall flat. And that tender mercy the Lord pours onto all of us is the same mercy He hopes we will pour onto others.

*Oh Lord, please give me the supernatural strength to
not only receive mercy but offer it to others. Amen.*

What Leads to Real Joy

*Distress that drives us to God does that. It turns us around.
It gets us back in the way of salvation. We never regret that
kind of pain. But those who let distress drive them away from
God are full of regrets, end up on a deathbed of regrets.*

2 Corinthians 7:10 msg

We live in a world packed with drama and infused with passionate and sometimes violent emotions, but one feeling that people flee from is guilt. Our world wants to avoid that emotion at all costs, since it's not a sentiment noted for its pleasure or joy. And yet no matter how people run from any signs of self-reproaching guilt, they come to know it intimately.

The question from 2 Corinthians 7:10 is "What kind of sorrowful distress do we have?" If it's the worldly kind that moves us away from God, then it leads to a deathbed of regrets. But if it is godly grief, then there is good news, for it turns our hearts around and leads us back to the way of salvation and God. And oh, how that godly sorrow leads us to real joy!

*Dear God, when I commit a transgression,
may I always have the godly grief that leads to
a repentant heart! In Jesus' name I pray, amen.*

The Light of Christ

"All this will be because the mercy of our God is very tender, and heaven's dawn is about to break upon us, to give light to those who sit in darkness and death's shadow, and to guide us to the path of peace."
LUKE 1:78–79 TLB

The starless sky became so shrouded in darkness you could barely see your hand in front of you. What a bleak night. Truth be known, sometimes you find your heart in a similar state of lightlessness. But even though your soul aches from turmoil and troubles, and all might seem lost, you are still confident that the dawn will arrive, where every shadow of hopelessness will be vanquished. Yes, that first light of daybreak—though it merely starts out as an ethereal glow on the horizon—grows in its luminosity and passion. Then suddenly that glorious ball of fire appears, spreading light into every shadowy fissure and cleft.

Daybreak is a daily event, and yet the sun's light changes our world like nothing else. The radiance of our Savior's light also changes our world—His divine presence illuminating every shadowy crevice of our souls. May we forever seek out and bask in the light of Christ. For it will guide us to the path of peace. And joy!

God, thank You not only for the light of our earthly sun but for the eternal light from Your only Son, Jesus! Amen.

Oh, the Plans I Have for Me!

*Do you want to be counted wise, to build a reputation
for wisdom? Here's what you do: Live well, live wisely, live
humbly. It's the way you live, not the way you talk, that counts.
Mean-spirited ambition isn't wisdom. Boasting that you are
wise isn't wisdom. Twisting the truth to make yourselves sound
wise isn't wisdom. It's the furthest thing from wisdom—it's
animal cunning, devilish conniving. Whenever you're trying
to look better than others or get the better of others, things
fall apart and everyone ends up at the others' throats.*
JAMES 3:13–16 MSG

Have you ever known a weasel? You know, people who are always
looking out for themselves? They are masters at manipulation. At
boasting. At scheming and twisting and lying. They have enough
vain ambition to fill an industrial-sized septic tank!

Back away from them. Don't light a match. This could be
dangerous. For the act of conniving is as deadly as it is devilish.
Hopefully that person is not you! But if you smell even a hint of
those sulfurous fumes on your soul, get help. Go to God. He'll
make sure you get back to living wisely and living well.

*Lord, sometimes I am not watching out for other people
because I am too focused on me and my dreams. Help
me to love and care for everyone like You would. Amen.*

Growing Up in the Lord

*Therefore, [let me warn you] beloved, knowing these things
beforehand, be on your guard so that you are not carried away
by the error of unprincipled men [who distort doctrine] and fall
from your own steadfastness [of mind, knowledge, truth, and
faith], but grow [spiritually mature] in the grace and knowledge
of our Lord and Savior Jesus Christ. To Him be glory (honor,
majesty, splendor), both now and to the day of eternity. Amen.*
2 PETER 3:17–18 AMP

Wolves—we've all heard the story of "Little Red Riding Hood."
Pretty scary story for kids, eh? Even adults could lose some sleep
over that gruesome bedtime tale. And yet there are plenty of real
folks out there who seem perfectly innocent and perhaps even
celebrated, but in reality they are crafty and misguided enough to
devour your innocence, lead you astray, or destroy you spiritually.
If any of the people you know are deceitful or corrupt or distort
the Gospel, beware of them. Seek the Lord on the matter, but it
might be best to pray for them at a distance rather than to spend
time in their company.

We are instead to stay steadfast in our faith and grow in the
grace and knowledge of our Lord and Savior, Jesus Christ.

*Lord, keep me steadfast in my faith, and
may I not be led astray by anyone! Amen.*

You're Not Alone

Dear friend, guard Clear Thinking and Common
Sense with your life; don't for a minute lose sight of them.
They'll keep your soul alive and well, they'll keep you fit
and attractive. You'll travel safely, you'll neither tire nor trip.
You'll take afternoon naps without a worry, you'll enjoy a good
night's sleep. No need to panic over alarms or surprises, or
predictions that doomsday's just around the corner, because
GOD will be right there with you; he'll keep you safe and sound.
PROVERBS 3:21–26 MSG

Do you sometimes feel that you're sleeping with one eye open
or maybe that you've been holding your breath for the last few
minutes or hours—or years? Do you have an undercurrent of
anxiousness that runs under your merry and confident facade? Do
you worry over doomsday predictions so much that you wonder
if some huge cosmic shoe is about to drop?

You're not alone in your fears, but take heart, you're also not
alone in the world. The Lord has promised to never leave you
or forsake you. God is right there with you no matter what. God
keeps His promises *always*. Know. Believe.

Almighty God, please help me to have clear
thinking and common sense when the world tries
to frighten me. Let me relax in Your mighty arms
of love and care. In Jesus' name I pray, amen.

Welcome the Joy!

For I am sure that neither death nor life, nor angels nor rulers, nor things present nor things to come, nor powers, nor height nor depth, nor anything else in all creation, will be able to separate us from the love of God in Christ Jesus our Lord.
ROMANS 8:38–39 ESV

You finally have the world by the tail—when suddenly your life falls apart. You thought you were highly valued at work, but they let you go without so much as an explanation. Your teenage son is told a series of lies about you, and he chooses to abandon you, never again coming home from college or even calling. You just ran a marathon and feel better than you've ever felt in your life, but your test comes back positive for Graves' disease. You celebrate your silver anniversary only to discover that your spouse has been unfaithful.

This world can be a harsh landscape to navigate emotionally and in every other way. Just when you think that you are loved and thriving, it can all be snatched away.

But the one hope we can cling to is that nothing can separate us from the love of God. Unlike humanity and its reckless promises and empty vows and fickle ways, God is unchanging. He loves you. Accept His gift. Welcome that joy!

Lord, when all the world abandons me, I thank You for Your great and unfaltering love. Amen.

Acknowledging the Giver

*Every good and perfect gift is from above, coming down
from the Father of the heavenly lights, who does
not change like shifting shadows.*

JAMES 1:17 NIV

Children love presents. Why not? They're fun to open, to stare at, to eat, to play with, to possess, and to share. And we love giving good gifts to our kids, right? But wouldn't it be horribly sad if our children went off to play with their toys and treats by themselves and never once thanked us or ever acted like they wanted to play with us or share in the overall joy that the presents were meant to bring? Of course, that would grieve us, and we would wonder what happened to their manners!

God gives us many good gifts, but sometimes we respond in the same way as those children. Our actions seem to say that we love the gifts more than we love the Giver. We don't always thank the Lord the way we should or seek His company when we want to enjoy the many gifts from His hand. But we too can change our manners in a heartbeat.

*Heavenly Father, I acknowledge that You are the Giver of all
good and perfect gifts. I thank You and praise You for them.
They are undeserved but lavish just like Your love. May You
and I always enjoy these wonderful gifts together.
In Jesus' holy name I pray, amen.*

The Apple of His Eye

"He found him in a desert land, and in the howling waste of the wilderness; he encircled him, he cared for him, he kept him as the apple of his eye."

DEUTERONOMY 32:10 ESV

These days people move at high speeds, not just in travel, but in other ways. And consequently, we no longer seem to have as much time for reflection, leisure time, or those "by still waters" moments the Bible talks about. But if we do turn off all the gadgets and find a slice of silence, we might begin to wonder about love and purpose and what is truly important in our lives. One question we might ask is "How does God feel about me?"

According to Deuteronomy, God encircles you and cares for you. You are the apple of God's eye! Really? You? Me? Yes. That is the God we love and serve. That is the God our souls have longed for.

So on days when the world hands you a howling wasteland, remember God's holy affections. Ponder them daily. Take them into the deepest part of you. Then allow the joy of it to shine from your heart and sing from your mouth.

Dear God, I am so happy to be the apple of Your eye. I love You too! Amen.

Doing Life with God

In his pride the wicked man does not seek him;
in all his thoughts there is no room for God.
PSALM 10:4 NIV

Maybe just one more peek in that full-length mirror, eh? Hair and makeup? Stellar, if you say so yourself. Nails? Electric dawn. That will shake things up a bit. You've got on your power suit with the retro shoulder pads. Yeah, baby. You give yourself a you-go-girl wink and then whisk yourself off to work where your uppers idolize you, your underlings fear you, and you're on your way up. Boy, does it feel good. But unfortunately, as that smug little smile lights up your face, pride is ever so slowly darkening your heart. Not such a great look.

God wants us to be happy but not by elbowing through life and knocking people down. The Lord wants us to do life with Him. There is an eternal difference between the two—one is holy and the other is wholly out of control. When the focus stays on us and only us, there is no room left for God. Without the Lord's daily presence, it's easy to let the world fill us with vanity and arrogance, which then lead to folly and sin.

Simply put—joy comes from doing life with God.

Lord, I want to always make room for You in my life.
In fact, I want You front and center! Amen.

Joy in Your Presence!

Through the victories you gave, his glory is great; you have bestowed on him splendor and majesty. Surely you have granted him unending blessings and made him glad with the joy of your presence. For the king trusts in the LORD; through the unfailing love of the Most High he will not be shaken.

PSALM 21:5–7 NIV

Mmm. The perfect day on earth. Let's see. A shoreline of white-gold sand that seems to stretch on forever. The mellow ebb and flow of the sea leaving behind treasures never before found. Some shells seem to whisper secrets from the depths. Little creatures, mystical in shape and iridescent in hue, wash in for a leisurely inspection. The breeze wafts in off the water like silk in your hair, and the sunbeams warm your skin. Your toes wiggle. Your heart soars. A day of pure happiness. And yet. . .

No joy on earth can compare to a single moment in the presence of God. Such resplendent radiance. Such unmatched beauty. Such unfathomable mystery. Such unmerited grace. Such extravagant love. Oh yes, I am made glad with the joy of Your presence!

Holy Father, I stand in awe of Your glory. You are awesome to behold. And yet I sense that You are not far away from me. Thank You for both Your majesty and Your faithful attentions. In Jesus' name I pray, amen.

The Gift of Friendship

*But Ruth replied, "Don't urge me to leave you or to
turn back from you. Where you go I will go, and where
you stay I will stay. Your people will be my people and
your God my God. Where you die I will die, and there I
will be buried. May the LORD deal with me, be it ever
so severely, if even death separates you and me."*

RUTH 1:16–17 NIV

One of the loveliest friendships portrayed in the Bible is the story
of Ruth and Naomi. When the time came for Naomi to return to
her homeland, one of Naomi's daughters-in-law—Ruth—refused
to leave her. Ruth said to Naomi the now famous lines, "Where
you go I will go. . .Your people will be my people." To enjoy the
rest of this heart-close relationship, spend some time reading
the book of Ruth.

God gives us the same gift of friendship today. That is, other
people who perhaps have similar temperaments and interests and
who desire to journey through life alongside us. These friends,
who help us in good times and bad, sometimes turn out to be true
treasures of the heart for a lifetime. They are God's gift of joy to us.

---

*Thank You, God, for the beautiful gift of friendship.
For those good and devoted people who
travel through life beside me. Amen.*

Forever Faithful

*And now I have it all—and keep getting more! The gifts
you sent with Epaphroditus were more than enough, like a
sweet-smelling sacrifice roasting on the altar, filling the air with
fragrance, pleasing God no end. You can be sure that God will
take care of everything you need, his generosity exceeding
even yours in the glory that pours from Jesus. Our God and
Father abounds in glory that just pours out into eternity. Yes.*
PHILIPPIANS 4:18–20 MSG

You planned this big church event—your parish's first high tea—as a community outreach. You made sure the tables were spectacularly set with fresh flowers and white linens. The sweet and savories could have been featured in a home-living magazine! And you managed to excite the local ladies not only to come to the function but to consider attending church in the future. All in all, God helped you make the affair a triumph.

Only one wrinkle—no one said, "Thank you." Or, "Great job." No one. Sigh. Don't you wish that when people forget to give you a much-needed good word, you could hand them a life script? It could include all the encouragement you need to bring you joy. But alas, there are no play scripts for life. Only people. But thank God, while humans can be fallible at times, the Lord is forever faithful!

Dear God, I am so glad You are true and trustworthy. Amen.

Beauty Arrived

*God sacrificed Jesus on the altar of the world to clear
that world of sin. Having faith in him sets us in the clear.
God decided on this course of action in full view of the
public—to set the world in the clear with himself through
the sacrifice of Jesus, finally taking care of the sins he had
so patiently endured. This is not only clear, but it's now—
this is current history! God sets things right. He also
makes it possible for us to live in his rightness.*
ROMANS 3:25–26 MSG

People love beautiful things, and one could say that we hold them up as a sign of goodness. But sometimes we don't do right when it comes to beauty. We trample it, abuse it, and spray it full of graffiti. We pollute God's earth, pervert the truth, and poison the air with cruel words. Perhaps splendor frightens us when it is placed alongside our sin.

Long ago, beauty and grace and love arrived on this earth—more than we've ever known or deserved—and we hung Him on a cross. But Christ's love for us is bigger than all our hate and sin combined. No man or king or demonic influence will ever be able to wipe away Christ's splendor or His legacy of grace.

When it comes to the ultimate beauty—Christ—may we never have a craving for destruction but only a desire for worship!

Lord, thank You for Your legacy of grace. Amen.

Run!

Strive for peace with everyone, and for the holiness without which no one will see the Lord. See to it that no one fails to obtain the grace of God; that no "root of bitterness" springs up and causes trouble, and by it many become defiled.

<small>HEBREWS 12:14–15 ESV</small>

In scary movies, sometimes there is an ominous note found by the heroine that tells her how to stay alive. The heroine slowly opens the note, and it contains one word—*RUN*! That is what we should do when our anger decides to take root in our souls. Yes, we're all going to get angry at some point, but we shouldn't allow it to thrive and grow. Anger can quickly turn into bitterness and hate, which is a sin. Yes, we've all had occasions when we can't seem to let go of a past offense, but remember that bitterness has nothing to do with bliss. Bitterness is only a burden.

Another good scripture to memorize is Ephesians 4:32 (ESV): "Be kind to one another, tenderhearted, forgiving one another, as God in Christ forgave you." That verse stings a bit since we too have sinned time and time again. Christ is wonderful to forgive us. May we do the same for others that we may never be caught in the spiritual peril that comes from bitterness. Instead, when we feel it stalking us—RUN!

Lord, help me to remember Your holy words about forgiveness. Amen.

The Lover of My Soul

"What man of you, having a hundred sheep, if he has lost one of them, does not leave the ninety-nine in the open country, and go after the one that is lost, until he finds it? And when he has found it, he lays it on his shoulders, rejoicing. And when he comes home, he calls together his friends and his neighbors, saying to them, 'Rejoice with me, for I have found my sheep that was lost.'"

LUKE 15:4–6 ESV

You have fallen head over heels in love, and you can barely breathe from the happiness of it all. It's such an achingly impossible yet beautiful feeling to love and to be loved that you find yourself smiling all the time because your heart is so full. Such sweetness and light. But what if your beloved left you—your heart would come undone with sorrow. You would think only of a tender reunion. You would do anything—move heaven and earth—to make things right again.

And so it goes with God. He is the Lover of your soul, and He will continue to pursue you—and He won't want to give you up. Yes, God desires that same tender reunion, so He moved heaven and earth for you. He went further than any lover ever could. His Son came to live among us and love us right into heaven. Won't you take His hand?

Lord, I love You, and I never want to be parted from You! Amen.

All the Yes-People

Faithful are the wounds of a friend [who corrects out
of love and concern], but the kisses of an enemy are
deceitful [because they serve his hidden agenda].
PROVERBS 27:6 AMP

Who doesn't like to hang out with a few of the yes-people? You know, the people at work who are paid to tell you that you're right all the time—even when you're not—or the other fawning and flattery folks who can't seem to say a word against you even when you're neck-deep in folly?

But to let yourself be led along blithely in life without restraint is like allowing the deceitful kisses of the enemy to lull you into thinking all is well—even when it's not. So beware of any complacency in your soul and any people who might be counseling you with a hidden agenda in mind. They will do you no good in the long run. In fact, they can do great harm to your soul. Instead, be happy to have a friend who is honest enough and wise enough and who cares enough to tell you the truth in love.

Holy Spirit, guide me away from all the yes-people in
my life who have a hidden agenda. May I always
be willing to listen to wise counsel. Amen.

Live Lavishly for Others

It is possible to give away and become richer! It is also possible to hold on too tightly and lose everything. Yes, the liberal man shall be rich! By watering others, he waters himself.
PROVERBS 11:24–25 TLB

You love your fine, bone china with the hand-painted pansies, but you never bother to get them out and actually use them. They just stay locked up in a display cabinet, getting dusty and maybe even going out of style. Same thing happens with so many of our treasures as we shelve them away in a closet or in the attic. Even pretty candles that get stored for too long may eventually melt a bit and go wonky.

When it comes to the talents that God has given to us, sometimes we hide those away as well for one reason or another. Over time they become a little wonky and unusable too.

Enjoying all that God has gifted us with requires a generosity of spirit. Yes, there will be chips and nicks along the way. There will be mess. It's life. But as your heart gives and pours itself out for others, it will be filled. What a joy-filled spiritual paradox!

Lord, help me to give lavishly to others, with my talents, my possessions, my life. Amen.

Tethered to His Heart

*For you were straying like sheep, but have now
returned to the Shepherd and Overseer of your souls.*
1 PETER 2:25 ESV

The old man's little fishing boat somehow got away and went adrift in the great lake. The elder gentleman felt grief over the loss, since it was his treasured possession and his joy. The townsfolk tried to help him retrieve the boat, but it was no use. They said that because it had been at the mercy of the wind and waves, it had now strayed too far from home. But after some time, when everyone else had forgotten—except for the old man—that little boat came bobbing right back to the same shore. The man sat in the boat and rejoiced in its return. People were amazed and told the tale to any newcomer. And when the strangers would ask how such a miraculous thing could be, folks always said that the little boat was tethered to the old man's heart.

Even as Christians we sometimes go adrift. We forget that we cannot navigate this stormy life alone. We forget how to pray and cry in repentance. We forget how to love Him and to be loved by Him—the One who has treasured us always.

But God is the Master of helping us remember who we are in Christ. Come home to Him—come home to joy!

*Oh Lord, thank You for keeping me
tethered to Your heart. Amen.*

That Mysterious Longing

He has made everything beautiful and appropriate in its time. He has also planted eternity [a sense of divine purpose] in the human heart [a mysterious longing which nothing under the sun can satisfy, except God]—yet man cannot find out (comprehend, grasp) what God has done (His overall plan) from the beginning to the end.

ECCLESIASTES 3:11 AMP

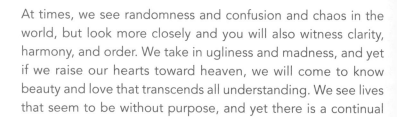

At times, we see randomness and confusion and chaos in the world, but look more closely and you will also witness clarity, harmony, and order. We take in ugliness and madness, and yet if we raise our hearts toward heaven, we will come to know beauty and love that transcends all understanding. We see lives that seem to be without purpose, and yet there is a continual divine stirring in the world that brings meaning and relevance to everything in its time.

And miraculously, eternity has been planted in our hearts—a mysterious longing that nothing can satisfy but God. We may feel that we are spinning uncontrollably in some strange terrestrial dance, but as Christians we have been made free in Christ, and with His supernatural help, we can become unbound from the unhappy confines of earthly sin. Even in the midst of what is still profound and unexplained, we can know that God has created a meaningful and joyful life for us now and for all time.

Lord, I praise You for beauty and love and purpose. Amen.

God's Good Gifts

I perceived that there is nothing better for them than
to be joyful and to do good as long as they live;
also that everyone should eat and drink and take
pleasure in all his toil—this is God's gift to man.
ECCLESIASTES 3:12–13 ESV

You get the kids off to school. You head off to work. Then you're back home to eat and do another round of unremarkable daily chores. You sigh and wonder, *When will I get to do something holy and beautiful for God?* But you're doing that right now. The writer of Ecclesiastes tells us that to eat and drink and find pleasure in one's toil is a gift from God. You don't have to be a volunteer nurse laboring in foreign lands or a worker in a local food pantry to do God's good work and enjoy His presence in your activities. If you're washing the windows at home, do it well, and know that God is with you. If you're creating a presentation for work, do it for the glory of God. When you cook up the family's favorite, make sure you invite the Lord to be at your table.

And as it also says in Ecclesiastes, may we remember to do good and to be joyful!

Lord, even if some of my tasks seem lowly, may I find
joy and Your holy happiness in all that I do! Amen.

The Tyrant of Gloat

Do not gloat when your enemy falls; when they stumble, do not let your heart rejoice, or the LORD will see and disapprove and turn his wrath away from them.
PROVERBS 24:17–18 NIV

The new neighbor is a real piece of work. His bouts of grumblings, intrusions, and bursts of testiness are not to be borne! He is a menace. *And*, you're not alone in your assessment of him. So when you hear that he's hurt his ankle while tripping around in your flowerbed, well, you're tempted to delight in his misery. Doesn't he deserve the pain? But then you remember that God loves you dearly, and that truth brings you to your knees. And too, you remember that gloating is not the merry sister to happiness. It might feel like happiness for a time, but the tyrant of gloat has turned on you too many times for you to be fooled again!

So what to do? You pray for the injured neighbor, and then you take him your best cheesy casserole. Yes, you had hoped the neighbor had changed and was suddenly a beacon of thankfulness when you arrived. But not yet. So you keep praying. Those prayers please God, and they bring you joy. And that joy will spill over onto the neighbor—for he may really be lonely and needy for heartbreaking reasons that no one knows but God.

Holy Spirit, when I am tempted to gloat,
remind me to pray. Amen.

Getting to Know You

But do not forget this one thing, dear friends:
With the Lord a day is like a thousand years,
and a thousand years are like a day.

2 PETER 3:8 NIV

The Bible speaks of eternity, and yet it is an unfathomable concept for our finite minds to deal with. This life is indeed but a brief flicker in the span of eternity, and so as Christians, wouldn't we want to get to know God better? A little like the way an engaged couple delights in discovering new things about each other before the wedding?

There are a number of ways to get to know the Lord better, such as being part of a Bible-believing fellowship, talking and listening to God, attending a Bible study, and going on church retreats. Psalm 23:6 (TLB) tells us, "Your goodness and unfailing kindness shall be with me all of my life, and afterwards I will live with you forever in your home." Yes, forever is in our future, and to spend it with God will be—well, pure heaven! May we enjoy getting to know the Lord's beauty and goodness and love as we wait for the glory of heaven.

Lord, I am finding joy in getting to know You.
I love every facet about You. Amen.

One of the Secrets

Now godliness with contentment is great gain.
For we brought nothing into this world, and it is
certain we can carry nothing out. And having food
and clothing, with these we shall be content.
1 TIMOTHY 6:6–8 NKJV

People are gatherers. Little things like doodads and knickknacks to fill the house. Big things to sit on and look at and enjoy. Clothes, big-kid gadgets, property, jewels, and cars. We make heaps and stockpiles and collections. And as fun and lovely as it all seems, we won't be able to take any of it with us when we die. Not one penny or doodad or toy. You might say, "Hey, that sounds kind of bleak!" It does, except from the perspective of a Christ follower. While it is true that we don't truly own any of our possessions—since we are merely passing through—we do get to experience the daily happiness of sharing them with God. He is the true owner of all things, and it is from His hand that we are blessed. God hopes that we will accept all those blessings from Him with a grateful heart, delight in them with Him, and share our bounty with others.

There lie several secrets to happiness.

Lord, thank You for sharing the wonder of Your earth with
me and for all the many blessings You bring into my life.
I accept them knowing we will enjoy them together,
and I will share them with others. Amen.

To Be Made Merry

You're cheating on God. If all you want is your own way,
flirting with the world every chance you get, you end up
enemies of God and his way. And do you suppose God
doesn't care? The proverb has it that "he's a fiercely jealous
lover." And what he gives in love is far better than anything
else you'll find. It's common knowledge that "God goes against
the willful proud; God gives grace to the willing humble."

JAMES 4:4–6 MSG

Women love fairy tales. What's not to love? You have good winning over evil. You have castles to dream about, feasts to pig out on, ugly frogs to gross out over, gorgeous gowns to die for, and knights to swoon over! You may even see a dragon or two just for fun. But most of all, there is that quintessential happily-ever-after. We love for everything that is wicked to be made right. For all things that are miserable to be made merry. For life to be noble again.

God wants a happily-ever-after too, and that is why He sent Christ. The Lord's honorable and self-sacrificing and splendid love is for everyone, but as with all princely offers, we must accept His beautiful proposal. Won't you say yes to the finest love your heart will ever know?

God, I accept Your proposal of love
both now and forevermore. Amen.

Clothe Yourself in Compassion

Therefore, as God's chosen people, holy and dearly loved, clothe yourselves with compassion, kindness, humility, gentleness and patience.

COLOSSIANS 3:12 NIV

The young woman just needed a break. She was lonely and cold, and she was on her last smile. She wandered into a coffee place to find a warm spot, but someone handed her a five and asked her to move on. She just looked a little too shabby—didn't quite fit in with the clientele.

And then suddenly out of the crowded coffeehouse, a much older woman came over and sat down beside the younger one as if she were her dearest friend. And so the management looked the other way, since she now had someone to come alongside her to say that she had value.

Years before, the older woman had also known poverty and loneliness, so she had learned how to clothe herself in compassion and how to befriend those in need. She had also come to know the joy that comes with kindness. In fact, her heart was overflowing.

Oh Lord, I am so grateful that You come alongside me as my dearest friend—that when I am on my last smile and dealing with my messiest day, You always say that I have value. Please help me to extend that same kind of compassion to all I meet. Amen.

Box of Illusions

But the serpent said to the woman, "You will not surely die. For God knows that when you eat of it your eyes will be opened, and you will be like God, knowing good and evil." So when the woman saw that the tree was good for food, and that it was a delight to the eyes, and that the tree was to be desired to make one wise, she took of its fruit and ate, and she also gave some to her husband who was with her, and he ate.

GENESIS 3:4–6 ESV

From the beginning, pride has been the fall of humankind. The serpent stirred up Adam and Eve's vanity to convince them they could be like the Creator who'd made them. And yet all that was wondrous and lovely and joyful in Eden was from God's hand. Arrogance is still one of the many tricks in the box of illusions that the enemy uses on us today. That box may look like it's full of happiness and light and treasures beyond our imaginings, but once opened and consumed, we discover that it was full of lies, darkness, and separation from God.

In the light of this knowledge, may we always choose to walk humbly with our Lord, for there is no one in heaven or on earth that can be brighter, or more beautiful, or more joyful!

*Lord, please forgive me for my prideful ways.
May I always walk humbly with You. Amen.*

Bad Trends

Once when we were going to the place of prayer, we were met by a female slave who had a spirit by which she predicted the future. She earned a great deal of money for her owners by fortune-telling. She followed Paul and the rest of us, shouting, "These men are servants of the Most High God, who are telling you the way to be saved." She kept this up for many days. Finally Paul became so annoyed that he turned around and said to the spirit, "In the name of Jesus Christ I command you to come out of her!" At that moment the spirit left her.

ACTS 16:16–18 NIV

Society loves a good trend, but some of them are deadly, such as the fad of seeking out the advice of a fortune-teller. The medium could be a fake, which means she'll grin all the way to the bank with your cash. Or the woman might be possessed by a demon and give you a glimpse of the future that you should not know or give you advice that you should not be hearing.

In both cases, it means we would not be trusting God. We wouldn't be relying on the Lord for His divine guidance or His everlasting joy and peace.

When we search for a happy future, may we always turn to God. He is the Master of happiness, for He is the One who created it.

Lord, may I trust in You always. Amen.

That Pure White Snowfall

Come, let's talk this over, says the Lord; no matter how
deep the stain of your sins, I can take it out and make you
as clean as freshly fallen snow. Even if you are stained
as red as crimson, I can make you white as wool!
ISAIAH 1:18 TLB

It started with just a few flurries of the white enchantment. The flakes of snow danced and swirled and tickled everyone's faces until there was nothing left to do but be merry and laugh. Then the flurries began to come down more heavily, embracing the people in a dreamlike cocoon of pristine wonder. What joy!

Yes, it is pure loveliness when that snow comes down all around us and blankets over the brown fields, the dead grass, and the grimy streets. Then what had been not so beautiful is transformed into newness and beauty. Yes, isn't it even lovelier still when the Lord takes our sins and miraculously makes them like the white of that pure and driven snow?

What goodness that You bring to our hearts, God!

I praise You, Almighty God, for Your mercy and for the grace
that came from Christ, which makes my many sins like the
freshly fallen snow. I thank You! In Jesus' holy name I pray, amen.

Those Blessed Peacemakers!

*"Blessed [spiritually calm with life-joy in God's favor]
are the makers and maintainers of peace, for they will
[express His character and] be called the sons of God."*
MATTHEW 5:9 AMP

School was out and the kids were home for the whole summer. What bliss—all day, every day, for the whole entire summer. Yay! But on day three, the young mother heard her kids bickering from the other room. Again. That squabbling had gone on until she was already at her wit's end. She wanted to scream, but instead she prayed. In exhaustion, she plopped herself down in the middle of the fiasco and quietly wept. The kids freaked out, of course, not knowing what to do with their mother. The children looked at each other, and in a moment of almost innocent bewilderment, they patted their mother on the back. Then she pulled them into a big hug. In that holy hush of a moment, the mom breathed a prayer of thanksgiving and told her kids a story about how getting along with people was one of the keys to happiness.

Was the summer perfect from that day forward? No, but the kids always remembered the quiet little story from their mom. They remembered what it looked like to be a peacemaker.

*Lord, I am not very good at being a peacemaker. Sometimes
I'm the one stirring up trouble. Forgive me and show me
how to be more gentle, wise, and peace-loving. Amen.*

Spreading Goodness

"Live out your God-created identity. Live generously and graciously toward others, the way God lives toward you."
MATTHEW 5:48 MSG

The party was fun, but still you waited for your friend to arrive. She always lit up the room. Not from gorgeous makeup, hair, and clothes—although she had some of that too—but because she was always swirling with light and merriment. She would ask about your life and then encourage you in some unique way. She spent more time spreading gracious words than talking about her latest accomplishments. She had a way about her. People automatically huddled around her because she made them smile. She made them remember that people could be truly fun and not just frivolous—that life had hope and that God was good.

Who are we at parties, or at work or church or home? Do we glide, or do people see us elbowing our way in? Do we spread goodness or gossip? Do people naturally gather around us, or are they slowly edging away toward the door. Yikes. May it never be!

Father God, I want to be a woman of grace and joy. My own efforts have come to nothing. With Your power, please show me how to live out my God-created identity and to live generously and graciously. I am willing to do life Your way! In Jesus' holy name I pray, amen.

Every Kind of Good Fruit

So we have not stopped praying for you since we first heard about you. We ask God to give you complete knowledge of his will and to give you spiritual wisdom and understanding. Then the way you live will always honor and please the Lord, and your lives will produce every kind of good fruit. All the while, you will grow as you learn to know God better and better.

COLOSSIANS 1:9–10 NLT

Mmmm. Someone sent you a wicker basket of fresh fruit. What a glorious gift—a golden container filled with goodies and all tied up with ribbons. Then you discover that it's not just a pretty presentation—the fruits are fully ripened and ready to eat. Let's see, there are luscious peaches, tart kiwis, creamy bananas, and plums so sweet they taste like candy. Ambrosia!

Oh, to be able to produce that kind of fruit as a Christian. Not just making a pretty presentation in the world, but being something excellent and satisfying—something that will bring people the goodness of God's truth and the sustenance of divine joy.

When the world tastes the fruit of a Christian, may it always be ambrosia!

Lord, may I produce good fruit in Your name.
I want to always honor and please You. Amen.

Finding Your Song Again

Serve the LORD with gladness and delight;
come before His presence with joyful singing.
PSALM 100:2 AMP

Some days you just feel broken down, and there's no fix in sight. Then when you read Psalm 100:2, you get more depressed, since you realize that you're way off track. Do you serve God with delight, and do you start the day with joyful singing? The reality is that in the morning you need two cups of strong coffee just to feel human again, and if you started singing too early, the neighbors in your apartment building will most certainly call the police. So what happens when the joy has seeped out of your spirit like helium from a day-old party balloon? You are left cynical and angry and empty. What now?

Psalm 91:14–15 (ESV) lovingly reminds us, "Because he holds fast to me in love, I will deliver him; I will protect him, because he knows my name. When he calls to me, I will answer him; I will be with him in trouble; I will rescue him and honor him."

God loves you, and He will rescue you and help you to find your song again. Call out to Him whenever you have need. Now is always a good time!

Lord, I don't know what went wrong, but I feel like
I'm falling to pieces. Please rescue me now. Amen.

209

Where Joy Knows No End

But our citizenship is in heaven, and from it we await
a Savior, the Lord Jesus Christ, who will transform our
lowly body to be like his glorious body, by the power
that enables him even to subject all things to himself.
PHILIPPIANS 3:20–21 ESV

When something painful or scary happens in our lives, we want to fast-forward to a happier time, don't we? For instance, if you find yourself in the middle of the labor and delivery of your first child, you may want to advance that life tape over to the wonderful part where you get to hold and cuddle your newborn. Yes!

Then when the really good stuff of life does happen, we want to push the PAUSE button or at least put the scene into slow motion. To make it last longer. Like getting a Swedish massage or a smoochy kiss from our beloved or savoring a Belgian chocolate truffle. Oh yeah.

But the promise of heaven is that there will be no need to fast-forward any event because there will be no suffering. There will be no need to slow anything down to make it last longer since time in eternity will last, well, forever. You will have all the time in the world for joy!

Lord, I thank You for the beautiful promise
of heaven where joy knows no end. Amen.

Religion Du Jour

We—every one of us—have strayed away like sheep!
We, who left God's paths to follow our own. Yet God
laid on him the guilt and sins of every one of us!
ISAIAH 53:6 TLB

In Old Testament times, the Israelites allowed themselves to be influenced by the neighboring peoples who indulged in pagan practices, and because of that sway, the Israelites did what was detestable in the sight of God. People worshipped the starry hosts. They burned incense to other gods. They sought omens and practiced divination. And they also engaged in other abominable rituals.

Today, because we're surrounded by religions from all over the world, some of these false belief systems have reshaped our culture, affected our everyday lives, and redirected our very souls. Sometimes we even dip into social media for the latest truism rather than consult our Bibles for God's truth. It makes a difference who we go to for guidance and help in our times of need. Who we worship and love. Who we praise for the good in our lives and where we find our joy.

We tend to change our spiritual tastes as if ordering up the soup of the day. In wisdom, we should ask ourselves, "What is my religion du jour? How has the world influenced me? Am I still the Christ follower I once was?"

Lord, I'm sorry for chasing after every kind of
faddish falsity. Lead me back to the simple
truth of Your Gospel message. Amen.

A Heart for Scheming

There are six things the LORD hates, seven that are detestable to him: haughty eyes, a lying tongue, hands that shed innocent blood, a heart that devises wicked schemes, feet that are quick to rush into evil.

The art of storytelling is simply wonderful. People truly enjoy a tale well told, whether they read it or watch it unfold on the screen. When the villain begins to weave his devious and dastardly schemes, we want to warn the characters. Stop! Run! There's a trap of some kind. We can see it all so clearly from our omniscient-like position on the couch. We can see that the dark scheming will ultimately end in misery, destruction, and maybe death. We are on the edge of our seats desperate to help the heroine—to make everything that is wrong into a right.

It's hard not to wonder if that is a little how God feels when He sees us going off on our own dangerous ways. God can see the trap, the abyss, the peril when we cannot. He is there warning us, guiding us, trying to keep us safe from the world, the enemy, and our sin. Whether we are willingly being taken in by a villain or we are the ones devising the wicked schemes, the Lord loves us enough to bring us back home. To make all that is wrong into a right.

Oh Lord, I choose to follow Your lead always! Amen.

Bringing God Delight

*God's Message: "Don't let the wise brag of their wisdom.
Don't let heroes brag of their exploits. Don't let the rich
brag of their riches. If you brag, brag of this and this only:
That you understand and know me. I'm God, and I act in
loyal love. I do what's right and set things right and fair,
and delight in those who do the same things.
These are my trademarks." God's Decree.*

JEREMIAH 9:23–24 MSG

People are on a constant hunt for happiness. We know just what we like. We indulge in spa treatments, culinary delicacies, not to mention those shopping sprees. Yes, we can be quite adept at bringing ourselves delight.

But what about God? He is the Creator of all things that are pleasant and beautiful and satisfying. Do we thank Him for the bounty? Do we ask Him to enjoy all of it with us? And do we ever consider how to please God—how to bring *Him* delight? Not as a way to work our way into heaven. That's impossible. But as a heartfelt thanks to the Lord for all He has done for us and because He is worthy of glory and honor and love as well as our faithful obedience. So today, what can you do to bring God delight?

---

*Dearest Lord Jesus, please let me live out
Jeremiah 9:24. Make it one of my life verses.
I genuinely want to please You. Amen.*

Our Waking Nightmares

"Be strong and courageous. Do not be afraid or terrified because of them, for the LORD your God goes with you; he will never leave you nor forsake you."

You wake up in a feverish sweat, gasping for breath. Your body is tangled in the sheets as if you'd been moving your legs trying to get away from something frightening—oh yes, the mountain lions. "It was only a dream," you whisper. You calm yourself, wipe your forehead, but suddenly you remember the realities of your waking life. Then a black flood of misery comes rushing in again, much worse than that nightmare. You have been abandoned by your spouse of thirty years, and even your friends seem to have distanced themselves from you in an effort not to take sides. You feel lost and alone with no way out.

Oh, what can you do with the many days and years ahead? How will you live with the suffering?

Cling to the promises of God. The Lord God loves you, and He goes with you. He's the God of the here and now. A God of might and power. Hold fast to Him. Call out to Him. Do not be afraid.

Father God, I come to You limp with sorrow. Be ever near me. Please help me. I need You now. In Jesus' name I pray, amen.

A Child of God

*Even in his own land and among his own people,
the Jews, he was not accepted. Only a few would
welcome and receive him. But to all who received him,
he gave the right to become children of God. All they
needed to do was to trust him to save them.*

JOHN 1:11–12 TLB

We are all desperate to be somebody, aren't we? In fact, people will stoop to ridiculous levels to feel as though they are truly exceptional. They do that name-dropping thing, not to mention one-upping their friends and colleagues. They exaggerate their skills, brag about their achievements, and boast of their exploits. Their friends are more illustrious, their adventures more swash-buckling. They are more traveled than others, more learned, more loved. They've even been guilty of gushing flattery on people just so they can hear the same glowing praises in return. Anything to be adored, validated, and set apart. But—can we not see the childish silliness of these games?

When you know the Lord, you no longer feel the need for these competitions. You are loved by God and you are His child. This knowledge is so freeing that you can spend more time being the exceptional woman God created you to be. And there is no prestige or accomplishment or joy on earth that is greater than being a child of God.

Lord, I am honored to be called Your child. Amen.

A Sacred Moment

"Are you tired? Worn out? Burned out on religion? Come to
me. Get away with me and you'll recover your life. I'll show
you how to take a real rest. Walk with me and work with
me—watch how I do it. Learn the unforced rhythms of grace.
I won't lay anything heavy or ill-fitting on you. Keep company
with me and you'll learn to live freely and lightly."
MATTHEW 11:28–30 MSG

Many Christians have heard that Christ's yoke is easy and His burden is light. But on dark days, we may whisper, "This is too much, Lord. I can't handle this burden."

Perhaps on those days you might ask yourself a little more about that heavy weight. Is it something from your past that you can't let go of, a lack of trust in God, believing the enemy's lies, or perhaps the consequences of your own sin?

Or maybe you feel as Job did, that the burden you carry is not your fault. Some things in this life are left as mysteries. And yet we are never left alone. When you walk with Christ and cast your cares on Him, there comes a sacred moment of trust, that He is the divine Keeper of your soul. Relish the freedom of such truth. Love the Giver of such sweet liberty. Hear Him say, "Follow Me and learn the unforced rhythms of grace."

Lord, may I always live inside that
sacred moment of trust. Amen.

Spiritual Landmarks

But grow [spiritually mature] in the grace and knowledge of our Lord and Savior Jesus Christ. To Him be glory (honor, majesty, splendor), both now and to the day of eternity. Amen.

2 PETER 3:18 AMP

When traveling, it's always nice to see a few familiar landmarks as you go along, so you can make sure you're still going the right way. It might be a brightly colored house that you pass on the highway, or a cozy café where you stopped for coffee once. Or when hiking, it might be a pebbly stream, a lofty pine, or a funky-shaped boulder. These earthly landmarks give you confidence, peace of mind, and even joy.

After you accept Christ and you go on your life journey with Him, there can be spiritual landmarks as you go along, such as that victory over a particular sin that had once been a stronghold in your life, an enlightenment of scripture, or that new longing to be in constant communion with the Lord.

Those spiritual landmarks of growth and maturity give us hope that we are on the right path. They also give a sense of confidence and peace and joy!

Dearest Lord Jesus, thank You for the spiritual landmarks in my life that show I am growing in the grace and knowledge of You. Amen.

The Greatest Joy of All

Jesus said to her, "I am the resurrection and the life. Whoever believes in me, though he die, yet shall he live, and everyone who lives and believes in me shall never die. Do you believe this?"
JOHN 11:25–26 ESV

It sure is easy to get off course. In our relationships. In our careers. In our dreams. In our attitudes and desires. In our walk with Christ. It's even easy to stray in our thoughts as we try to focus on prayer rather than that grocery list! Then while we're wandering off in no-man's-land, the world likes to throw things at us like we're some kind of target in a carnival game. We get hit with confusion, pain, doubts, exhaustion, depression, grief, failure, loneliness, and a host of other horrors.

No matter what happens to us or how far we stray, may we always head back to the cross. It's where we can find peace. The death and resurrection of Jesus Christ for the forgiveness of sins was the most sorrowful event in history, and yet the most joyful too.

The question we are left with is the same now as it was back then. Jesus asked Martha, but He also asks you, "Do you believe this?"

Lord Jesus, my answer is yes. You are the resurrection and the life. I believe! Amen.

I Choose Joy!

*Jesus continued: "There was a man who had two sons.
The younger one said to his father, 'Father, give me my share
of the estate.' So he divided his property between them."*
LUKE 15:11–12 NIV

People are notorious for wanting what they want when they want it. The story of the prodigal son illustrates this point well. The wayward son didn't want to wait until his father's death to enjoy his inheritance. He wanted it. Right. This. Minute. And so, his father gave in. And as was expected, the young man squandered his newfound wealth in wild living. At last, the young man came to his senses and wanted to go home.

Modern people have a similar problem. We want lots of *presents* from God, but we don't always desire God's *presence* in our lives. We want our inheritance in the kingdom but not necessarily the everyday company of our Lord. But both of these joys come together.

The story of the prodigal son has a happy ending, and it is the same ending the Lord wants for all of us. May we all choose to go home. May we all choose the presence as well as the presents of God. May we all choose joy!

---

*Lord, I'm grateful that You are a forgiving Father and that You
welcome me back home with much celebration. Amen.*

Piece by Pretty Piece

*Who will transform our lowly body to be like
his glorious body, by the power that enables
him even to subject all things to himself.*
PHILIPPIANS 3:21 ESV

A mosaic can be so amazing when it's finished, but to see it in the creation process might not be so satisfying. Up close, as one begins, it might even look like a mess. But if you pull back far enough, you can see the overall design. You can see a picture coming together. As piece by pretty piece falls into place, you see the hint of something heavenly, joyful, and eternally beautiful taking shape before you.

That is our hope in Christ.

As Christians, someday when we die, we are promised glorified bodies, but the Lord wants to start this beautification process right now. Day by day, piece by pretty piece, won't you let Him put His masterful touch on the mosaic of your soul? He is ready to create something truly remarkable, something heavenly with your life.

---

*Every day, oh Lord, I desire to become more and
more like You. Piece by piece I want my soul to
become a work of art that reflects Your divine beauty,
truth, and love. May my words elevate You and my
life exalt You. Praise be to Your holy name! Amen.*

In tribute to our mighty God,
may we live our days in thanksgiving,
close our days in prayer,
and rise up with shouts of joy!

Anita Higman, an award-winning author from Texas, has fifty books published, and she has a BA in the combined fields of speech communication, psychology, and art. A few of Anita's favorite things are fairy-tale castles, steampunk clothes, traveling, antiquing, exotic teas, laughing around the dinner table with family and friends, and gardening—although most of the time she has no idea what she's doing! Please drop by Anita's website at anitahigman.com. She would love to hear from you!

More Inspiration and Encouragement

How God Grows a Woman of Confidence

Featuring two hundred–plus devotional readings complemented by scripture selections and prayers, this lovely collection offers a powerful blend of inspiration, encouragement, and assurance for every area of your life. Touching on topics like beauty, prayer, God's Word, family, friendship, trust, and more, you will find yourself drawn ever closer to your heavenly Father as you meditate on each reading and open your heart and mind to God's Word.

Hardback / 978-1-68322-883-7 / $12.99

National Cold Storage Company

Also by Harvey Shapiro

Harvey Shapiro

National Cold Storage Company

New and Selected Poems

 Wesleyan University Press
Middletown, Connecticut

55.9445

The poems in Part I appeared in *The Eye,* published by Alan Swallow in 1953, in *Mountain, Fire, Thornbush,* published by Alan Swallow in 1961, and in *Battle Report,* published by Wesleyan University Press in 1966. Those in Part II appeared in *This World,* published by Wesleyan University Press in 1971. Those in Part III appeared in *Lauds & Nightsounds,* published by SUN in 1978. Those in Part IV appeared in *The Light Holds,* published by Wesleyan University Press in 1984. Some of the poems in Part V have previously appeared in the following publications: *Images; The New Criterion; Partisan Review; Pequod; Poetry East; Poetry Flash.* "Cynthia" was first published in *The Quarterly,* Volume I, Spring 1987.

All inquiries and permissions requests should be addressed to the Publisher, Wesleyan University Press, 110 Mt. Vernon Street, Middletown, Connecticut 06457

LIBRARY OF CONGRESS CATALOGING-IN-PUBLICATION DATA
Shapiro, Harvey.
 National cold storage company: new and selected poems/Harvey Shapiro.—1st ed.
 p. cm.
 ISBN 0-8195-2152-3 ISBN 0-8195-1153-6 (pbk.)
 1. Title.
PS3537.H264N3 1988
811'.52—dc19   87-20472
              CIP

Manufactured in the United States of America

First Edition

Wesleyan Poetry

Contents

1. Battle Report

2. This World

3. Lauds and Nightsounds

4. The Light Holds

5. New Poems

1. Battle Report

From THE EYE

The Heart

In the midst of words your wordless image
Marches through the precincts of my night
And all the structures of my language lie undone:
The bright cathedrals clatter, and the moon-
Topped spires break their stalk.
Sprawled before that raid, I watch the towns
Go under. And in the waiting dark, I loose
Like marbles spinning from a child
The crazed and hooded creatures of the heart.

Summer

The glazed day crumbles to its fall
Upon the tiny rout of fishing
Boats. Gulls convey it down,
Lengthening their cries that soon
Will rake the evening air; while some,
Silhouetted on a strand
In a jumbled line of target ducks,
Watch as ebb tide drains the bay.

From a rotted log upon
The shore, like the other beached
Mutations, shell and weed, I wait
For Highland Light to cast its eye.

July unhives its heaven in
A swarm of stars above my head.
And at my feet, flat to the water
That it rides, the lighthouse beam,
A broken spar, breaks its pulse.

"What have I learned of word or line?"
Ticks on, ticks off; ticks on, ticks off.
The bay, that was a clotted eye,
Is turned to water by the dark.
Only my summer breaks upon
The sea, the gulls, the narrow land.

Power in America

The struck animal, blurred
By subsequent hours, lies
Upon the road, hunched fur and spirit.
At night, drawn by the hum of power,
Then doubled into pain, sight smashed,
It caught the radicals of
Descending speed, their brilliance.

Or the boy in Dreiser's novel,
That blind head, felled
By the big city hotel,
Its monolithic shine and scramble.
Even Crane, who tried to make
A shining steel structure of a bridge
Lead him out, caught by the brilliance
That kills, in America.

As at the movie's close,
Man alone, against the wall,
Watches the lights move in,
The fugitive, hatless there.
And we, thrilled into our fear,
See the enormously wheeled clatter,
Glistening, never in error,
Rise to break his back.

Death of a Grandmother

Let me borrow her corpse a little.
Over that clown in finest linen,
Over that white-dressed dummy, pretty girl
(Dressed for a party, the daughters cried),
Let me speak a line.

The dead lie in a ditch of fear,
In an earth wound, in an old mouth
That has sucked them there.
My grandmother drank tea, and wailed
As if the Wailing Wall kissed her head
Beside the kitchen window;
While the flaking, green-boxed radio
Retailed in Yiddish song
And heartache all day long.
Or laughter found her,
The sly, sexual humor of the grave.

Yet after her years of dragging leg,
Of yellowed sight,
She still found pain enough
To polish off the final hours with a shriek.
To what sweet kingdom do the old Jews go?
Now mourned by her radio and bed,
She wishes me health and children,
Who am her inheritor.

I sing her a song of praise.
She meddled with my childhood
Like a witch, and I can meet her
Curse for curse in that slum heaven where we go
When this American dream is spent—
To give her a crust of bread, a little love.

From MOUNTAIN, FIRE, THORNBUSH

Adoration of the Moon

for Max Weber

Sappho's moist lotus and the scudding moon
Speak to each other in a dilation upon Acheron.
Lean out of the abyss of origin four ragged Jews,
Masters of wrath and judgment, gentled by the moon.
Their tall hats rise, their faces lengthen
As O the spell is on them. Three grip
The word for ballast, while the fourth,
Beard upended, sniffs the moon-fleck as it falls.
Support them in flight, goddess,
That when the darkness comes, thy light put out,
Their candle's flame send up in steep aroma
The scholar's must.

The Talker

from a Midrash

While all the choiring angels cried:
Creation's crown is set awry!
God fabled man before he was,
And boasting of His enterprise
Bade angels say the simple names
That mark in place each bird and beast.

But they were dumb, as He foretold—
When man stepped from the shuddering dust
And lightly tossed the syllables,
And said his own name, quick as dirt.
Then angels crept into their spheres,
And dirt, and bird, and beast were his.

Mountain, Fire, Thornbush

How everything gets tamed.
The pronominal outcry, as if uttered in ecstasy,
Is turned to syntax. We are
Only a step from discursive prose
When the voice speaks from the thornbush.
Mountain, fire, and thornbush.
Supplied only with these, even that aniconic Jew
Could spell mystery. But there must be
Narrative. The people must get to the mountain.
Doors must open and close.
How to savor the savagery of Egyptians,
Who betrayed the names of their gods
To demons, and tore the hair
From their godheads
As lotus blossoms are pulled out of the pool.

The Prophet Announces

On an illustration from an
eighteenth-century Haggadah

And so they arrive for all the world to see,
Elijah with the shofar to his mouth,
His hand upon the guide reins of the King,
Who rides an ass. They look so sad.
In all, a quiet scene, unless the shofar's sound
I barely hear was louder in that century.
Behind them is a tree, and on its branch
A startled bird, to say there's hope of life.
Old images of immortality.
But where's new Adam come to greet the King?
Unless this be the moment of their setting out,
And no one's heard that death's been done and even
Now the first light's traveling from the east.

Feast of the Ram's Horn

As seventh sign, the antique heavens show
A pair of scales. And Jews, no less antique,
Hear the ram-rod summons beat their heels,
Until they stand together in mock show
As if they meant to recognize a king.

For they are come again to this good turning:
That from the mountain where their leader goes,
In ten days' time they greet the Law descending.
And these are ancient stories from a book
That circulates, and for them has no ending.

All stand as witness to the great event.
Ezra, their scribe, before the water gate
Takes up the book, and the people rise.
And those who weep upon the word are bid
To hold their peace because the day is holy.

Feast of the ram's horn. Let the player rise.
And may the sound of that bent instrument,
In the seventh month, before the seventh gate,
Speak for all the living and the dead,
And tell creation it is memorized.

Let Isaac be remembered in the ram
That when the great horn sounds, and all are come,
These who now are gathered as one man
Shall be gathered again. Set the bright
Scales in the sky until that judgment's done.

Spirit of Rabbi Nachman

"The word moves a bit of air,
And this the next, until it reaches
The man who receives the word of his friend
And receives his soul therein
And is therein awakened"—
Rabbi Nachman's preachment on the word,
Which I gloomily thumb
Wondering how it is with me
That I am not yet on the first
Rung (and many with me!).
To move a bit of air!

If a man ask, can he have
This thing, whether it be
An infusion of soul, or souls,
Steadfast to complete the journeying?
Words moving a bit of air
So that the whole morning moves.

From BATTLE REPORT

Battle Report

1

The Adriatic was no sailor's sea.
We raced above that water for our lives
Hoping the green curve of Italy
Would take us in. Rank, meaningless fire

That had no other object but our life
Raged in the stunned engine. I acquired
From the scene that flickered like a silent film
New perspective on the days of man.

Now the aviators, primed for flight,
Gave to the blue expanse can after can
Of calibers, armored clothes, all
The rich paraphernalia of our war.

Death in a hungry instant took us in.
He touched me where my lifeblood danced
And said, the cold water is an ample grin
For all your twenty years.

Monotone and flawless, the blue sky
Shows to my watching face this afternoon
The chilled signal of our victory.
Again the lost plane drums home.

2

No violence rode in the glistening chamber.
For the gunner the world was unhinged.
Abstract as a drinker and single
He hunched to his task, the dumb show
Of surgical fighters, while flak, impersonal,
Beat at the floor that he stood on.

The diamond in his eye was fear;
It barely flickered.
From target to target he rode.
The images froze, the flak hardly mattered.
Europe rolled to its murderous knees
Under the sex of guns and of cannon.

In an absence of pain he continued,
The oxygen misting his veins like summer.
The bomber's long sleep and the cry of the gunner,
Who knows that the unseen mime in his blood
Will startle to terror,
Years later, when love matters.

3

My pilot dreamed of death before he died.
That stumbling Texas boy
Grew cold before the end, and told
The bombardier, who told us all.
We worried while we slept.
And when he died, on that dark morning
Over Italy in clouds,
We clapped him into dirt.
We counted it for enmity
That he had fraternized with death.
From hand to hand
We passed in wonderment
The quicksilver of our lives.

4

I turn my rubber face to the blue square
Given me to trace the fighters
As they weave their frost, and see
Within this sky the traffic
Fierce and heavy for the day:
All those who stumbling home at dark
Found their names fixed
Beside a numbered Fort, and heard
At dawn the sirens rattling the night away,

And rose to that cold resurrection
And are now gathered over Italy.

In this slow dream's rehearsal,
Again I am the death-instructed kid,
Gun in its cradle, sun at my back,
Cities below me without sound.
That tensed, corrugated hose
Feeding to my face the air of substance,
I face the mirroring past.
We swarm the skies, determined armies,
To seek the war's end, the silence stealing,
The mind grown hesitant as breath.

News of the World

The past, like so many bad poems,
Waits to be reordered,
And the future needs reordering too.
Rain dampens the brick,
And the house sends up its smell
Of smoke and lives—
My own funk the major part.
Angling for direction,
I think of the favored in Homer,
Who in a dream, a council meeting,
At the bottom of despair,
Heard the voice of a god or goddess,
Though it was, say, only Polites
Speaking. Turning to a friend,
I ask again
For news of the world.

Monday

Everybody thinks the past is real.
The window and the skull
Admit light. The past comes through
Like that—undifferentiated,
Hallucinatory, of no weight.
Sleepless that night, he saw the
Room close-woven, a nest
Of chairs, tables, rug
The past was filtering through.
It had no odor, no
Emotion. You could not
Say that in the silences
The past came in
Like water over sand.
There was no movement.
You could not draw the blind.

Past Time

I believe we came together
Out of ignorance not love,
Both being shy and hunted in the city.
In the hot summer, touching each other,
Amazed at how love could come
Like a waterfall, with frightening force
And bruising sleep. Waking at noon,
Touching each other for direction,
Out of ignorance not love.

Sunday Morning

You begin to tell a story.
I perceive it is to be
Another of those unpunctuated excursions
Into the country of my failures.
You, pointing to the familiar landmarks.
I, nodding in assent.
We settle back.

ABC of Culture

So the angel of death whistles Mozart
(As we knew he would)
Bicycling amid the smoke of Auschwitz,
The Jews of Auschwitz,
In the great museum of Western Art.

The Night

Memory, my own prince of disaster,
My ancient of night.
In the scored silence
I see the dead.
They file past the fixed camera—
The ritual wave, and the smile,
And good night. For an instant
They are there, caught
In their clothes and their gestures;
White faces glow
In the murk of the film,
Absurdly alive. How little I own
This family of the dead,
Who are now part of night.
Memory, my own prince of disaster,
When you go,
Where's the night?

The Six Hundred Thousand Letters

The day like blank paper
Being pulled from my typewriter.
With the six
Hundred thousand letters of the Law
Surrounding me,
Not one of them in place.

Beyond the Demonic Element

I cast out
Beyond the demonic element
And the fear of death
Into that bright water
Beyond this water
Where leviathan swims.
Communication is instant
When it comes—close
As my hand, the words on my tongue,
Though the crying in my ear
Is my own death crying.

The Old Nostalgia

"The Night the Old Nostalgia
Burned Down" is
The most beautiful
Title in American writing.
Every night I visit it—
Crammed full of heroes,
Blondes, girls out of
My own childhood and the neighborhood.
Tenderly I light the flesh
And watch it go, like dreams:
Mother and father burning down
To the sweet music
Of Stephen Foster, hymned
In the P.S. 3 assembly.
Every day is a new beginning,
The charred remains
Softening the scent of bleak
December; background music
Against which criss-cross
Rapid images of a new life.
I leave the scene
Confident the spectacle
Has enduring worth,
Will light me a long way,
Songs to sing.

National Cold Storage Company

The National Cold Storage Company contains
More things than you can dream of.
Hard by the Brooklyn Bridge it stands
In a litter of freight cars,
Tugs to one side; the other, the traffic
Of the Long Island Expressway.
I myself have dropped into it in seven years
Midnight tossings, plans for escape, the shakes.
Add this to the national total—
Grant's tomb, the Civil War, Arlington,
The young President dead.
Above the warehouse and beneath the stars
The poets creep on the harp of the Bridge.
But see,
They fall into the National Cold Storage Company
One by one. The wind off the river is too cold,
Or the times too rough, or the Bridge
Is not a harp at all. Or maybe
A monstrous birth inside the warehouse
Must be fed by everything—ships, poems,
Stars, all the years of our lives.

2. This World

For W C W

Now they are trying to make you
The genital thug, leader
Of the new black shirts—
Masculinity over all!
I remember you after the stroke
(Which stroke? I don't remember which stroke.)
Afraid to be left by Flossie
In a hotel lobby, crying out
To her not to leave you
For a minute. Cracked open
And nothing but womanish milk
In the hole. Only a year
Before that we were banging
On the door for a girl to open,
To both of us. Cracked,
Broken. Fear
Slaughtering the brightness
Of your face, stroke and
Counterstroke, repeated and
Repeated, for anyone to see.
And now, grandmotherly,
You stare from the cover
Of your selected poems—
The only face you could compose
In the end. As if having
Written of love better than any poet
Of our time, you stepped over
To that side for peace.
What valleys, William, to retrace
In memory, after the masculine mountains,
What long and splendid valleys.

Days and Nights

1

You keep beating me down.
When I reach a balance,
You break it, always
Clawing for the heart.
In the electric light
We face each other.
Whatever you want of me,
Goddess of insomnia and pure form,
It's not these messages I scratch out
Morning after morning
To turn you off.

2

Whether I had room
For all that joy
In my economy
Is another matter.
Rejecting me,
She shut out all my light,
Showed to me the backs
Of houses, tail lights
Going fast,
Smiles disappearing.
Every man
Was my enemy.
So it was for many a day.
I could not
Climb out of it,
So close was I
To her will.

3

"He that is wise may correct natures."
Alchemy. The philosophical stone.
Your shadow over the page.
Your hair to my cheek.

Your eyes great riding lights
In the alcoholic storm that now
I remember, along with that
Bruising sweat of rhetoric
I thought appropriate to the times.
He that is wise
May have his life to remember.
But I am reduced to reciting
The letters of the alphabet.
If I say them with fervor
(Saying them with fervor)
Will memory be stirred?
Your own goddess-voice
In the leaves, in the night
Of the body, as I turn the page.

4

Well, it was only Bottom's dream—
Methought I was and
Methought I had.
Outside, the sky is a field
In which the seeds of minerals shine.
And I am hunched over the board
On which I write my nights
Breathing configurations
On the winter air. As far from you
As ever I was far from you.
The cold locks everything in place.
Now I am here. The flame of my match
Everything that is given to me.

5

Suddenly I see your face close up
And all my senses scramble
To get the shock
Home again. In sleep
Not knowing who I am
Or however that spent match struck.

6

The white brilliance under the eyelids
So that all things appear to me
In that color. The worlds you see
Exist in joy. Eyes like doves.
Equilibrium, a white brilliance.

7

Now you come again
Like a very patient ghost,
Offering me Zen records,
A discourse on the stomach
As the seat of the soul,
Your long white neck to kiss.
The tiger's eye that is
Your favorite jewel
Shines in your hand.
Wanting to, I can't conjure
You up, not a touch.
Unbidden, you cross a thousand miles
To say, This is the gift
I was going to give you forever.

Sister

My dead sister dreams away her life.
About forty years of dreaming
As I count.
My father blamed my mother
For the child's death
And wasn't at the funeral.
The tears, the tears she bred
In me out of my sister's loss,
Weeping of hurt, deprivation, age,
The insanity of life.
My sister, eager for her share,
Under such a tiny headstone
In a city we never pass.
Kin, dreaming dark poems
That spill into my life.

From Martin Buber

"A story must be told in such a way
That it constitutes help in itself."
Or not the way telephone addicts
Trap themselves for eternity
In a recital of symptoms—
Blood pressure, urine, sleep—
Saying tonight what they will
Relive tomorrow.

(Finding you whole
After a night of hatred
World to my touch
Like bread to my touch
Which I ceaselessly crumble
And the loaf is there.)

(Or when the traffic slurs
Early in the morning
Of a long night
And I strike it rich
With calm.)

The Synagogue on Kane Street

Anachronisms are pleasant.
I like shifting periods
As the young rabbi doesn't shift tones
Saying "The Ethics of Maimonides"
And "The Reader's Digest."

There is no reason for survival.
As we drift outward
The tribal gods wave farewell.

It is the mother synagogue of Brooklyn.
We are a handful in a cathedral.

When I was asked
I said the blessing
For the reading of the scroll
Almost correctly.

The reader had a silver pointer.

The parchment before me
Was like a beginning.

Riverside Drive

from the Yiddish of Joseph Rolnick

Pulling myself out of bed,
I leave the house.
The blueness caresses me.
The wind pushes my hair.
A whole world of quiet
I fill with my steps
On the sidewalk,
And in the street,
The milkman's horse.
Somewhere, on a higher floor,
Along a dark corridor,
The milkman makes his shining rows.
Running, the papers
Under my arm,
I don't look at numbers.
I know the way
Like the horse.
The sun is already up
On the east side of the city.
Its flames, its grace
Spill, whole canfuls, on the cliffs
Of the Jersey shore.
At 310 Riverside Drive
A man on a low balcony,
Young but with mustache and beard—
His appearance not of here—
Stretches a hand toward
The west and shouts
Something like, See there!
And I stand like him
With my papers raised
Like an offering
To the light.
The two of us
Come for the first time
To this place,
To the red cliffs
Of this morning.

Ditty

Where did the Jewish god go?
Up the chimney flues.
Who saw him go?
Six million souls.
How did he go?
All so still
As dew from the grass.

The Kingdom

Battering at the door
Of a pretend house
With pretend cries
Of rage and loss
As I sit remembering
Quiet
And dead white.

The Way

Why are you crying in Israel,
Brother? I ask as I switch over
To the emergency oxygen.
Do we have to dig up all
The Freudian plumbing
To reconstruct our lives?
If I had clean air like you
I think I could breathe.
As it is my mouthpiece keeps
Clogging and my eyes blur.
I can barely make it
Between the desks.
And you, walking
Between orange trees
Among the companions,
And still so far from the way.

Where I Am Now

Every morning I look
Into the world
And there is no renewal.
Every night, my lids clamped,
I concentrate
On the renewal to come.

I am on the lookout for
A great illumining,
Prepared to recognize it
Instantly and put it to use
Even among the desks
And chairs of the office, should
It come between nine and five.

To the Teacher

That the galaxy is a river of light
That the order of seeds is in my hand
I ask to enter this world without confusion.

The enormous lights
And mysteries of this world
Which the teacher says
I shut from myself
With a hand,
Spending my sight
On these snarled lines,
This closed-in town
Where I walk and work
And find you in sleep
In the dark room, the dark town,
In a life that I cannot
Honestly call the way.

He has been asking for help
Everywhere for his child
With the clogged tongue.
Not that the boy
Should speak with eloquence.
But that he should speak
His need—to the world,
The citizens. The barest
Speech. I am happy.
I am sad.
The sense is beautiful.

The reader begins
With the destruction of the city.
It is the same tune
Every day for a week now.
But how he appears to enjoy
That rattle of words.
Crowds fleeing, others
Looting shops
In the most expensive
Avenues of the city.

Smoke like a cowl
Over the words
And the reader's body.
He must experience it
To the end
Each day, as it was set down
From the roots of heaven.

In the sequence
The angel of each verse
Stands like a point of flame.

A Message from Rabbi Nachman

The extra-human
Swarms with disciples.
Like worms
Tumbling out of the Book of Creation,
The Book of Splendor.
Each with a light
In his head.
But smeared with
The contemplation of ecstasy.

Kabbalah—
A transmission
From mouth to ear.
The words of my friend
Steady my world
Even as I say them.

There are stones—
How else will the house
Be built—
Like souls
That are flung down
In the streets.

For Delmore Schwartz

1

How do they go on living?
How does anyone go on living?
A woman kills her three children
In 1954. In 1966 she kills
Another three. And the husband
Continues to go to work
At the same job. Which
Is to be judged insane?
And we keep walking the same
Roads, past mayhem, slaughter
Of innocents—this morning, the granny
Curled up beside her bottle
Of Petri wine at a side door
Of the Paramount—every day,
Leading sensible lives.
The sirens seem never to stop,
Even in the country, amid
Crickets or ocean sound.
What we all know,
What keeps humming in the back
Of the brain. When the language
Pauses, the killing begins.

2

Your intelligence was so clear
In your first poems, like
Mozart in his music.
Yet it could not help you,
As you said,
When the old arguments,
The din around the family table,
Grew louder all about you—
The arguments we endlessly rehearse
When mind loses its own motion.
Then our jaws lock into the face
We had, on the words we said
Under our breath, to ourselves,

To our underselves, so fiercely deep
They were for years beyond hearing,
And now do all the talking.

3

Disturbed by dreams,
I wake into the chilled morning.
The dreams are rich
With patterns of rejection
(Mother, Wife), suicide and loss.
A victim of such disasters,
When I awake I judge myself
Harshly and long.
Four A.M. on a vacation morning.
The surf takes over in my head, a running
Commentary, a Greek chorus,
Saying something like, nothing but the sea.
In my universe of feeling,
I can hear the sea. These dreams,
Bits of genre, Viennese pastry,
From which I awake, stuffed
With bourgeois living, these dreams
Of the dead fathers I believe in . . .

3. Lauds and Night-sounds

Through the Boroughs

I hear the music from the street
Every night. Sequestered at my desk,
My luminous hand finding the dark words.
Hard, very hard. And the music
From car radios is so effortless.
And so I strive to join my music
To that music. So that
The air will carry my voice down
The block, across the bridge,
Through the boroughs where people I love
Can hear my voice, saying to them
Through the music that their lives
Are speaking to them now, as mine to me.

The Intensity

When you think over what she said and what you said
The spaces begin to get larger until they modulate
Into silence. You stand there staring at each other
With no balloons floating the words, no
Captions, only the intensity of sight making
A language to scare anyone interested in communication
Or believing that two human beings can connect.

Which is why my happiness on the subway brings me
    back
To myself after last night's trouble. The body warmth,
The distended-with-sleep faces, the memories
Of Hart Crane riding this line, tunneling this way
Under the river that is east. Next time
When I beg for something, will you recognize
Need, stop talking, stop closing the door.

Notes at 46

1

What distinguishes our work
Is an American desperation.
Who thought to find this
In the new world?

2

I owe my father a tribute.
On his last day
When the head nurse
Asked what he wanted
He said, I want to
Look into the eyes of a young girl.

The eyes of a young girl.
I want to look into
The eyes of a young girl.

3

It's nothing to me
Who gathers us in.
And it's nothing to me
Who owns us now.

I can think of Venice
Or Jerusalem.

Armand's little goat beard
Quivers in the spring.

4

It suddenly strikes me
That at forty-six
I want to write the lyrics
Of a boy of twenty
So I blow my brains out.

5

Not wanting to invent emotion
I pursued the flat literal,
Saying wife, children, job
Over and over.
When the words took on
Emotion I changed their order.
In this way, I reached daylight
About midnight.

6

"I wish I had never been born!"
He shouts at six.
A pure despair.
At forty-six I cannot say that
With honesty.
Pure passion is beyond me.
Everything is mixed.
Grief allied with joy—
That he is able to say it!

7

In October the house is chill.
Still, the cricket of summer
Sings, reminding us of promises.
As long as the heart listens
It pumps blood.

Riding Westward

It's holiday night
And crazy Jews are on the road,
Finished with fasting and high on prayer.
On either side of the Long Island Expressway
The lights go spinning
Like the twin ends of my tallis.
I hope I can make it to Utopia Parkway
Where my father lies at the end of his road.
And then home to Brooklyn.
Jews, departure from the law
Is equivalent to death.
Shades, we greet each other.
Darkly, on the Long Island Expressway,
Where I say my own prayers for the dead,
Crowded in Queens, remembered in Queens,
As far away as Brooklyn. Cemeteries
Break against the City like seas,
A white froth of tombstones
Or like schools of herring, still desperate
To escape the angel of death.
Entering the City, you have to say
Memorial prayers as he slides overhead
Looking something like my father approaching
The Ark as the gates close on the Day of Atonement
Here in the car and in Queens and in Brooklyn.

For the Yiddish Singers in the Lakewood Hotels of My Childhood

I don't want to be sheltered here.
I don't want to keep crawling back
To this page, saying to myself,
This is what I have.

I never wanted to make
Sentimental music in the Brill Building.
It's not the voice of Frank Sinatra
I hear.

To be a Jew in Manhattan
Doesn't have to be this.
These lights flung like farfel.
These golden girls.

Saul's Progress

I told my son:
"Stop trying to screw the monkey's tail
Into his bellybutton.
Originality
Is never its own
Justification.
Some innovations
Get nowhere."

"The Sunday monkeys are my friends,"
He said.
I was on my way down
From the heavenly city
Of the 18th-century philosophers.
He was on his way up,
Almost three.

2

"Moby Dick is smarter than
The other dicks."
A song to make the
Bad guys happy.
You sang it all day Saturday
With snot-filled nose
And clouded eye,
To raise me
To a fury.

3

You sit on the crest of a dune
Facing the sea,
Which is beyond sight.
Your anger at me
Makes you play by yourself,
Tell stories to yourself,
Fling out your hurt
To the wide sky's healing.

A red boat in one hand,
A blue in the other,
You begin singing songs
About the weather.
Cliff swallow, brilliant skimmer.

4

As if he were me, he comes bounding in,
All happiness. I owe him
All happiness. For these years at least.
When he smiles and says, a good time,
I have no notion who else
He has made happy with my happiness.

Muse Poem

While I'm waiting for the words,
Could you just
Lean over me a little,
That way,
With your breasts
Of imagination, incense,
And blue dawns.

It is always the same quiet night.
You in your desperation say,
"What you are writing is poetry.
No one will read it."
You worry about my health
When I find I am not
To be famous. But I am
Already inside you in my thoughts.

City Portrait

Her husband didn't give her highs,
Just made her lows less low.
Said, with the lips trembling.
Breasts too, I think.
Beautiful woman.
Going to bed with strangers now.
Trying to think it all out.
On the west side of Manhattan,
Twelve floors above the murderous streets.

In the Room

Seeing the figure of that man
Caught in a murderous hatred,
I wept for him openly
Before the children,
And I write of him in a low style
But touching on elevated things.

In the room
Nothing has happened
Yet the two of them
Stand apart, watching a ship
Wreck, a wild storm,
Their own blood drumming.

Her hatred of him
Makes her eyes shine,
Brings color to the points
Of her fingers and her hair.

Before we knew about urban poetry
I opened the door and found you
Bathing in the sink, on Stanton Street—
1949—your skin still gleaming.

I can't sleep.
Love has fixed my head.
Now this girl, now that.

Who needs this tumult?
I ask myself,
So proud of the hours
I spend staring.

Muse,
Once you made this chaos shine.

A Notebook

At the bare edge
The images seem fabulous.

I certainly didn't
Wear myself out
With brilliance.

"It is forbidden to be old" (Nachman).

If you steam-blast the bricks
In Brooklyn, they will
Come up as bright as Henry James.

Dead Indians are in the underbrush
Waiting for the word.

I don't like you
And I don't know
Anyone else.

The stars be hid
That led me to this pain.

I stroke my wife's angel hair
Thinking of you.

It is a bowl of blue light.
It will be there all day
Now that I have seen it.

I take out my old anxieties
And they still work.

A notebook of dry cunts.

Why is everything discussed
With that high cackle?
Ladies, I weep for beauty
And you bear it.

I used to visit bombed-out towns.
Now I visit bombed-out people.
There's a kind of beautiful smell
To both, which I can't
Put out of my mind.

Man, the master of choice.

Words, rushing into judgment.

All right, you mother stickers,
This is a fuck up.

Musical Shuttle

Night, expositor of love.
Seeing the sky for the first time
That year, I watched the summer constellations
Hang in air: Scorpio with
Half of heaven in his tail.
Breath, tissue of air, cat's cradle.
I walked the shore
Where cold rocks mourned in water
Like the planets lost in air.
Ocean was a low sound.
The gatekeeper suddenly gone,
Whatever the heart cried
Voice tied to dark sound.
The shuttle went way back then,
Hooking me up to the first song
That ever chimed in my head.
Under a sky gone slick with stars,
The aria tumbling forth:
Bird and star.
However those cadences
Rocked me in the learning years,
However that soft death sang—
Of star become a bird's pulse,
Of the spanned distances
Where the bird's breath eddied forth—
I recovered the lost ground.
The bird's throat
Bare as the sand on which I walked.
Love in his season
Had moved me with that song.

Tight Like That

Who can refuse to live his own life?
A spray of leaves in the lamplight.
A saxophone on the dark street.
Like the forties. In those days
For the price of a pitcher of beer
You could spend Saturday afternoon
Listening to the exchanges,
The deep guttural stirrings
Of so much light and dark.
At the corner of Fifty-second
At the break at the Downbeat
We saw Billie draped in fur,
Gardenia in her hair.
Bless you, children, she said.
Whatever became of the music
I drank to at Nick's bar,
Pee Wee Russell's clarinet
Jammed into Brunes's belly,
Shaking like his sister Kate.
Hunkering down into my own story,
I begin to see it all close up,
Just under the pavement.

The Bridge

for John Wissemann

John, the old bunker fleet at Greenport
Is a ghost. Many beautiful things are gone.
The masts, the dockside buildings
Float in your blue water colors,
Blue and black, in Brooklyn,
Where I seem to be giving up the ghost.
Artists of the region. All one island.
Whitman's crummy fish-shaped island.

Like you I do the indigenous stuff—
Crabs from the creek, blues from the September sea,
Poems from the tar roofs, and the redbrick library
Where they house the prints—opening the Bridge!
Fireworks and exultation! Crowds moving
In a mighty congress back and forth.
While we, unmoving on the starry grid of America,
Stare failure in the face, our blazing star.

It was a dream of summer. From the cliffs above
The Sound—hummingbirds hovering, red foxes
At the door—at evening I could see the schools
Of blues come in, savaging the waters and the bait.
Everything I wrote was magic to me. Ancient days.
Believe me, John, they wear us down with shit and work.
But one pure line—still mine or yours
For the grasping—can take us to that farther shore.

47th Street

In the delicatessen
The countermen
Were bantering about the messiah,
Lifting the mounds of corned beef
And tongue. He wouldn't come,
They said, you couldn't
Count on it. Meaning:
They would die in harness.

Nightsounds

1

The joy of her hair
On his cock
Lit up the whole morning.

2

My fingers bear the marks
Of fishhooks, puppy bites,
All the sweet bites of the actual.

You, goddess, who grab me
Between the second drink and the third,
I now see like me
For the marks I carry on me.

3

As if the night were a problem
I had to crack
To let the dawn through.

4

It is near bedtime
And suddenly I am stunned
By the gold
Of the whiskey in my glass.
I cannot understand
Why so much has been given.

5

He was looking for a
Universal message, like
Hemorrhoid sufferers
You are not alone.

6

You throw one leg
Over the covers.
A gleam of snatch
In the half light.

7

I have long been a man
Of filthy habits.
And now in middle age
They give me pleasure.

8

I am watching another
Man's defeat.
It seems
He cannot bring himself
To it
While I watch.

9

Where you stand
There stand all the worlds.

10

What is this sweetness
I am overcome by
As if I had earned
My rest.

Domestic Matters

It wasn't what I had thought—
Children taking up
Most of the house, leaving
Me (or so it often seems)
Only room enough
For the bed. Which itself
Is a kind of relic, as if
From an earlier
Marriage. And so you turn
In the bedroom door,
White, and so small,
To say good night.
To say there are
Two of us.

I am crying over this body of yours
Which is to wither in the dust.
Already your belly's thrust outpoints
Your breasts. The hair of your head
Grows thin. A skeleton
Smiles to me with your gums.

We are almost
Out of earshot
Of one another
Yet our answers
Seem to find
Connected questions
Of an urgency
So deep, they might
Be coming
From the center
Of a life.

We were comrades
In a disastrous war.
We have created a history
That will be sung
In the psyche of others.
Troy's burning
And the flames may light us
All the way to death.

Cry of the Small Rabbits

The cry of the small rabbits facing death.
Nobody would want to sing like that.
A short, high wailing. So what
If death gave them voice to sing?
I face my own rage and fear, tearing for words
That I can say calmly in sentences
That will not stop. I want to see
The next line glitter, and the last
Come crashing like surf.

The Realization

If one could follow a man
Through the places of his exile,
Asking him at each point
Why he had strayed from his life
Or been turned from it,
In time the dialogue
Would be meaningless
For the exile would be the life.
So we live.

Vacation Poetry

An inexhaustible day but in the end
There were no prizes. I sharpened
Into seeing a few times, before
And after whiskey. The beach was
One great sunlit navel.
The sea, like a medieval gloss, moved
On four levels. I walked east along
The tide mark, the spent text.

This air is made of bird calls,
Telephone wires, blue sky and clouds.
It has a disarming honesty. Peanut butter
Would not spread as evenly.
I have come to think of my daydreams of you,
Seventeen porno movies with one plot,
As a waste of time. The longitudes
Of my indifference begin to envelop space.

How difficult it is to acknowledge
This is what I'm here for. A furniture
Mover might have a stronger sense of mission.
In combat I understood the value of survival
And the necessity for strict attention.
In life's miasma, I drift apart.
Even when she looks toward me
My moves tend to be comical.

"The great elementary principle of pleasure"
By which man "knows and feels, and lives, and moves."
I'll drink to that, said Brustein,
Smacking his lips. For the fourth time today
I swim in the sea. Butterflies pass me
On my bike, as do bikinied women,
Strutting in their cream and brown. Voluptuous
Pages from Keats and Baudelaire.

From a Chinese Master

1

If you want to enter the room
You have to say something. You cannot
Take it for granted that you have already
Entered the room. This I want
To point out to you with a smile.

2

Early Sunday. Under the phosphor glare
Birds sing merrily, twigs bud.
A dream pushed me from my bed
Breathing of promise like this April.
Believe me, said the teacher in my dream,
A single true gesture, if it be
Only that of the big toe, is enough.

3

The glamor of death is on their heads.
Wanderers in the anthologies.
After the job I sit with beer and bourbon.
In what cold light shall we be one?

4

At the start and at the finish
What we want
Is to be close to the living,
Our heads against the skin of the song.

4. The Light Holds

July

You poets of the Late T'ang send me messages this
   morning.
The eastern sky is streaked with red.
Linkages of bird song make a floating chain.
In a corner of the world, walled in by ocean and sky,
I can look back on so many destructive days and nights,
and forward too, ego demons as far as mind reaches.
Here, for a moment, the light holds.

May 14, 1978

The poet Kenji Miyazawa asks me,
What world is it you want to enter?
Percussive rain on the early morning window.
The house, the steady breathing, focused now
on the lighted surface of my desk.
I cannot answer him for joy and dread.

City

Silver dawn over Madison Avenue.
The refrigerator shuts softly, like a kiss.

He is dying of the terminal cutesies,
she says of the cultural journalist,
the newspaper spread before her on the table.
Thousands fail in her sight daily.

The word "happiness"
like the sun in late March
is a light I can see
but not feel. There it is
on the back of my hand
as real as my hand
clenched now
against the wind on 48th Street.

In Great Neck, at 4:30 in the morning,
Ring Lardner and Scott Fitzgerald
walk the streets. American success
is their theme. The sleepers drink it in
across the lawns.

In the lamp's circle,
warmed by bourbon,
I play the role out. It is
not to tell the world
anything. What is it
the world would want to know?

Her furious body, plunged into sleep.
On the pillow, her live hair,
helmet and cloak. What I say in the room
is for me and the walls. We are doing darkness,
each in his own way.

Middle Class

Whatever happened to the screaming-meemies?
I see my life has surfaced once again.
She explained to me on the phone
all the things I had to live for.
It came to three items. Not enough.
I spent one hour with one son at his shrink
discussing (my choice) why he seemed to hate me.
Because I'm insensitive and unfeeling, he said.
The shrink said it wasn't hate but anger.
We all agreed to discuss it again.
If I get up when the alarm rings tomorrow,
I can pay for the hour and all the hours.
On the subway I see nobody finds it easy.
As beautiful as you are, you're not enough.

Cummings

On May nights, in Patchin Place,
Greenwich Village of my memory,
girls from Smith and Vassar
vagabonding for the weekend,
lovely in the alley light,
would chant up to the shy poet's
window: How do you like your blue-
eyed boy, Mr. Death? And indeed
Buffalo Bill's defunct—pencil-thin
by the alley gate, sketchbook in hand,
open collar of the artist, across
from the Women's House of Detention
in the waning light of afternoons.

The Gift of Remembering

1

Judy Handler's mother said
I looked like the butcher's son.
Peter Geiger, my rival,
died in the war. I survived,
flying over Germany, looking
more Jewish than ever.

The hard-boiled egg I eat
still has the sweet sustenance
of an egg taken from a glass jar
on a bar in Atlantic City
in 1945, the summer after
my war had ended, my missions done,
and the drinks all on the house,
whoever paid.

2

Rain and a low sky bring the planes in close
though not as close as they came to our tents
in Italy, on dark days, friendly fighters
practicing their rolls, to tell the sleeping grounded
combat crews, this is the sound of friendly death.

3

Fire on the rim of heaven.
Two bright stars off the wing, higher,
and the cities underneath,
cold, final blaze.

Brooklyn Heights

1

I'm on Water Street in Brooklyn,
between the Brooklyn Bridge
and the Manhattan Bridge,
the high charge of their traffic
filling the empty street.
Abandoned warehouses
on either side.
In the shadowed doorways, shades
of Melville and Murder Incorporated.
Five o'clock October light.
Jets and gulls in the fleecy sky.
Climbing the hill to Columbia Heights,
I turn to see the cordage
of the Brooklyn Bridge, and behind it
the battle-gray Manhattan.

2

This room shelved high with books
echoes with my midnights. Pages
of useless lines swim in it. Only
now and then a voice cuts through
saying something right: No sound
is dissonant which tells of life.
The gaudy ensigns of this life
flash in the streets; a December light,
whipped by wind, is at the windows.
Even now the English poets are in the street,
Keats and Coleridge on Hicks Street,
heading for the Bridge. Swayed aloft there,
the lower bay before them, they can
bring me back my City line by line.

Blue Eyes

Young women with the baby fat
still on them, smelling of milk.
Against that, her bravery—
striding out of bed in the morning,
her years, her children underfoot,
her blue eyes flashing warning.

"I could make some of these guys very happy,"
she said, looking up from the personals
in the *New York Review of Books*.

You read to her of war,
devastation, gut-chilling
insecurity, and her blue eyes
waver, and she sleeps
like an American child.

"Is this a peak experience?"
she said, sliding down beside him,
her blue eyes laughing at his desperate age.

Sound of surf through dense fog.
Moisture streaming from the screened windows.
"Where are the beautiful love poems?"
she keeps asking him.

She became the line
he had in his head
just before sleep, that
he thought he would retain
and now it's gone.

Interlude

He had his own prescription for entering
the life of his times.
This was what everything drifted to,
inexorably: His hand
on the small of her back.

She spoke about the special
loneliness of the city.

She said, lay down your arms, nothing
will come of this but more tears, more
unhappiness, on which you fatten and grow dull.
Enjoy the streets. The rain is
your proper element. Stop trying to light fires
where damp ashes are what is meant.

Goddess, destroyer, flaming-haired,
whiskey-throated,
the small birds keep their distance
when you walk across to me.

Cityscape

The self hurt, humiliated,
has no recourse but to the world.
Dawn's light
on the streets, though
the buildings are still dark.

Sparrows nesting in the hollow crossbar
of the traffic light. A beak
and head emerge, and then the line
of flight, as if city air
could sustain flight.

June and the hum of air conditioners
fills the side streets.
A poster in a Madison Avenue boutique
says Poverty Sucks. The crowd
coming out of the Whitney opening
believe it, so well kept
they shine along the pavement.

Gulls as far inland
as Fifth Avenue.

After the garbage truck
has stopped grinding the world,
the rhetoric inside my head
catches and begins to work.

My eye on the cityscape,
nervous, alert,
as I move through
the day. No part
of the surface
is neutral ground.

The End

Imagine your own death.
I'm wearing my father's
gray tweed overcoat.
I've just had a corned-beef
sandwich on 47th Street

(I asked for lean
and it came fat,
I should have sent it
back) when it hits me
in the chest.

A Jerusalem Notebook

I

A city of ascensions,
nowhere to go but up.
Forcing the spirit in New York
is the commonplace; we live
there as if we were in Jerusalem,
Jesus and Mohammed touching down
and going up, just another
launching pad, as I get off
the bus and head home.

2 *Postcard*

It is not far from here
that the parents stood
and the child, placed into the priest's machine,
heard the wail
of Moloch. And the bronze god,
arms outstretched, smiled at the smoke.
Two of the kings of Judah
burned their sons here—
Hell, Gehenna, Gai Hinnom,
the pleasant valley of Hinnom,
pink, scarred and silent
in the fading light.

3 *Tourists*

She is crying over three olives
that I threw out. Three olives
but my food, she cries. She is
not a child but a woman.
Outside Zion Gate, Jaffa Gate,
Dung Gate, she rubs my arm slowly.
Gates excite her. Where I come in
at night, the city is so beautiful.

4

It is the temple mount.
It is a little like the temple mount,
though I myself constitute
the sightseers, worshippers,
and sometimes the visiting god.

5

Whatever brought me here, to a new moon
over Zion's hill, dark moon
with the thin cusp silvered,
help me believe in my happiness, for
it was guilt that woke me. A voice
on the telephone crying breakdown.
Illusions of my own ego causing destruction
while outside the marvelous
machinery of day has opened, light
traffic on the road to the citadel.
And as I look again, it is all
swept clean, except for
a faint pink in the sky and on the old
stones of the city, and language in my head
that I brought with me, that I carry,
that I use to mark my way.

6

My way of being in the world:
not perfect freedom or the pitch
of madness, but that the particulars
of my life become manifest
to me walking these dark streets.

7 *For C R*

When I dropped permanence from my back
and saw what I had taken for
solid buildings and good roads
was desert all about me and within me,

how bright became the sunlight,
how sweet the evening air.

8 *The Old Jewish Poet Floats in the Dead Sea*

It is the lowest place on earth
but he has been lower.
For example, he has been on the heights
of Masada, watching the Roman soldiers
jack off in the baths below.
He knows his turn will be next.
Beneath him floats a crow.
Beneath the crow floats the crow's shadow.
Beneath the crow's shadow is another Jew.
These Judean junk hills
fill his head with sulphur.
Every hill is a hill of skulls.

9

I understand we are like smoke.
It streams from my cigar into the morning air,
silken, prismlike in sunlight
as I sit by the window.
Nothing I do with my life
could be as beautiful.

10

Lizard lines in his skin.
Striving to become one with the stones
like the lizard, even as the pen
darts into the shadow of the page.

11

I have dreams coming out of my ears,
she said. Why not? This city has seen
so many mad dreamers, their stale dreams
even now looking for new homes.
The stones dream in the sun,
the lizards. In the golden mosque,

riots of line and color, shapes dream
in the marble columns, pulsing in
and out of sleep. When the city wakes
the action is brief and bloody.
Let it sleep. Let the gaberdined Jews
dream of the Messiah. He approaches
the blocked-off gate of the walled city.
Taste the dream of the Jews.

12

Why did I want to sit out all the time,
was the air so special? Yes,
soft and today dust-blue. But the smell
of corpses had been everywhere, and more to come.
Red buses and blue buses raced the roads
to the small towns, carrying infant Jesuses,
dynamite. Blondes from Scandinavia,
silver-toed, tried on Arab dresses
while the man in the stall scratched his crotch.
It was all happening inside the city.
And at the edge was desert.

13

Middle East music on the radio: Hebrew love songs,
Arab wails. Carmel Dry Gin
taking me up Zion's hill.
Lights on the stones of the ancient city.

14

Who needs more happiness? People living
on the edge (of pain, of death,
of revelation) need time in the sun,
a lengthening interval between
the sonic boom and the rattled glass.

15

I cannot dissever my happiness from language
or from your body. Light a candle for me

at the false tomb of David, I am of that line.
Let the young scarecrow who might be from 47th Street
say a blessing for me. Sway over the candle's flame
like the old Arab riding toward me on his donkey.
If I forget my happiness, let me be dust.
Jerusalem, here I am going up again.
It is your moon, your labyrinths, your desert
crowding east where the sun waits.

5. New Poems

Tides

His wanting her, and the sea
has not lost its intensity,
though tonight its still surface
is like dull slate facing luminous sky.
Beyond the breakwater, everything happens.
The excitement is the same, catches him up
in her small room by the harbor.
White houses, blue shutters, weeping willows
like fountains in the backyards.
Cod, haddock lifted from the depths
on the party boat. The North Atlantic
breathes on him, even in the subway
under the East River, on his way
to work, his image of her raised
legs, lifted sex, and the sullen
tides, inexorable, timing him.

History

1

It was his own scream he heard in the act,
center stage, ego driven, self-expressed.

Her fingers, extravagantly wild.
Dragon Lady. Lurid. Night colors
of deep red, black.

2

You spread the lines, six lines,
on the glass tabletop. This was
our evening at home.

I am not even permitted to call you.
It upsets you, you said, it
leaves you depressed.

Cloth of gold, you sat opposite me,
open and vulnerable, the foreplay
of eyes and speaking tongue.

Observations

1

At Yaddo, 1949,
W. C. Williams tells me
about this guy
who shot himself
while on the phone
to his girl: "You see," says Bill,
"he was a muff-diver."

2

Has there ever been a useful critic?
Longinus, of course, whose text
preserves lines by Sappho.

3

She had his scalp on her belt.
He had her voice in his poems.

4

Studiously third person,
weighted down with family angst,
suddenly in his *Education*
Henry Adams notices
"the frail wreck of the grasshopper summer."
He has touched his childhood
with his manhood.

Two Cornell Deaths

Because I live I must search these graves.
Coming out of Patchin Place onto 10th Street,
past the iron gate, the figure of Cummings
slouching there, the women ranged
along the street, heads craned
to the barred windows, now silent,
of the Women's House of Detention,
I go to have a drink with Charlie Weir.

He was writing mysteries, working on a novel,
toiling in the wardrobe room of NBC.
In Ithaca he had sometimes missed his classes.
When the train rounded the bend,
hurrying to New York, he flung
his blue books on the tracks, then
marked the grades. For which he was sacked.
Reputed to be a brilliant teacher.

The facts mean nothing in the light of day.
What was the caliber of the weapon?
Partying in Ithaca, thin Jack Sessions
in the corner, another ghost.
He wrote the story of a blind man
who recovered his sight and found
his wife impossibly ugly. She
whom he had loved. What was
the caliber of his weapon, and what other
damage did he do? Last spotted
in a restaurant in the Village.

Pain leaks into this December light.
I take these ghosts with me wherever I go,
asking them, Why now? Why this moment?
Because the liquor is inexhaustible,
the girls will stand at the bar
and smile at the stories, as they used to do.
If you walk by the river, Manhattan
is like a book, the pages turn,
the words march down those pages.

Look back to the lights along the river.
Wait for the dark, wait for the city to come on,
windows and bridges blazing.
Whatever you needed was there, wasn't it?

From an Autobiography

I was conceived on the night
of my sister's funeral.
As a replacement, I suspect.
But she was very beautiful,
my mother said, and when I was born
I was quite ugly, with a large bump
on my head, so large the attending doctor first
advised surgery. My grandmother
insisted she could do the job
with the flat of a kitchen knife,
using almost constant pressure.
And so it turned out. My mother,
when she saw me said, Why did God
take away my beautiful child and give me
this ugly baby instead? And she turned away,
not to touch me
for the first few months of my life.
This is family history.
What is unclear is my father's role.
Was the night of my sister's funeral
a suitable time for making love?
Did they both think that?
Or was my father excited by my mother's grief?
Though I honor my mother and father,
I want to ask a few more questions.
When I was very young I heard my mother say
(though she later denied it when I used
the information in a poem) that my father,
blaming her for my sister's death,
did not attend the funeral.
My mother, against his advice,
had taken my sister to visit a sick cousin.
This was 1923. Whooping cough was the killer.
My father has been dead for 16 years,
my mother for two. Among her effects,
I found a large photograph I had never seen before.
In it she is holding my sister, who is
indeed beautiful. My mother is 20 in the picture
and very happy, almost serene,
she whose anxiety is with me still.

Comment

Stepin Fetchit—this is from
his obituary in the *Times*—justifying
his life, the eyeball rolling
he had done for his movie pay,
spoke of Bill Cosby and Sidney Poitier:
"I set up thrones for them to come
and sit on." A noble quote, like
"We are, in midmost ground, our own dead kings."
Blackmur's iambic roll to it.
That he, down the long avenue, could
find himself, in purple stuff, leading the way.

Autobiography

The clouded sky over Brooklyn
made his meditations shapely.

Fire escapes with pigeons on them.
A leafy street.

Moments when life
tended to make sense.

Earlier, when the kids
were young, taking them to the beach.

Appetite, as in the crow's cry.
Searching the bright shards.

Curtains

Equipped with an imagination for disaster,
you never seem to anticipate the real disasters.
They leave you stunned, with no second line
of defense. Then, after days or weeks,
you begin to celebrate them, reciting inwardly
their advantages, how they free up
the imagination for a while. Not that what happened
was exactly falling-down funny. No,
it was like curtains in the colorful world of death.

Last Things

Is it a failure of my imagination
that I cannot believe in the end of the world.
Or that I believe in it, quietly, as I do in death
but in its own good time. Though, of course,
I understand the weapons are at hand, madmen are loose.
People I loved were concerned, are concerned.
I drift off into the orbit of my own troubles
finding them more familiar, I suppose, though
also more immediately painful. I think
I have made my choice. Others must make theirs.
Nothing can be done to coerce the unwilling
or to safeguard them or us if our dreams
project dragons reeling across a waste of sky.

Cynthia

When I take off your red sweatpants,
sliding them over the ass I love,
the fat thighs, and now my hands
are trembling, my tongue is muzzy,
a fire runs under my skin.

Cynthia's red-gold muff caught
the morning light as she strode from my bed,
upright and proud. Her body was
a vehicle for pleasure. It had carried us
into sleep as if we were children,
protected forever from the void and dark.

She slept with him
if at dinner he pleased
her. If he did not, she
did not. She was free
to choose, without
the drags of love.

Every day I wonder about you—
why it is your eyes look so wild
sometimes. Other times, so naked,
so pure-blue naked. Your shields, you say,
speaking of your diaphragm, your contact lenses.
Nevertheless, you think of yourself as being at home
in this world in a way I am not.
I understand it is my myth-making intelligence
gets me in trouble, makes me want to fix you
as earth nourisher, source of comfort,
when it is what is lost and erratic in you
brings you to my bed, beatings against fate
or circumstance, stabbings toward transcendence
that leave us both bruised and happy in ourselves.

To be with her
was to be in a cloud
of sexual joy—hair, eyes,

speech. The merest
flick of her tongue
on a word set off
resonances.

I fell in love with
one of the poisonous tomatoes of America.

Mind-fucking at 3 A.M.
because where are you
and that's where you are.

At the instant of her coming, she makes a throaty sound.
It is back beyond words, low in the throat,
away from the tongue. I never try to translate it,
any more than I would translate sunlight or deep shade.

Before sleep, C in my arms, her back toward me,
puts my right hand on her left breast. If I
could make an amulet of that.

She is beautiful to me
as she wakes from sleep,
sits straight up—
force, energy, and purpose
in her straight spine.

I wonder where her cunt is tonight
and her proud head. She did
make me happy, more than once.
One Sunday morning, light everywhere
in the living room, she on the couch
facing me, garbed in my blue bathrobe,
one breast shapely through the opening
of the robe while I drink my coffee, happy.

The last time
I went down on Cynthia
was the last time
though her petals
in the rose red light

She said she had taken on seven students the previous
night on her visit upstate, and that all had watched,
masturbating as each colleague performed. One had her
in the missionary position, one took her from behind,
one made her ride on top, one came in her mouth, one
had her lean over a table, one did her on his lap, one fucked
her up the ass. The last to have her, she said, because
he had come six times, had trouble achieving an erection.
After she had told all this to her lover, fiction or fact,
he became the eighth man.

There'll always be room for you
in my capacious vagina, she said.
At the elevator door. Some parting!
("Capacious quiff" would have been catchier.)

All the questions she asked him
he answered from another life.

He was trying to understand
the nature of the pain.
Maybe when a woman
aborts a child
it is like this: killing
something in oneself.
Someone else has already done
the killing, yet there
is more left to kill.

She was hidden in his thought
like a tick in a dog's fur.
He could feel the rise with his finger
where her mouth sucked blood.

Combat

In the war in which I fought
not all my actions were heroic.
I remember particularly the time
I bargained with God—the plane
seemed to be going down,
smoke filled the cabin—
if he would only get me out alive,
I would . . . What was my promise,
my heartfelt vow? Tears in my eyes,
probably, and trembling. I might
have been speaking to a woman.

Italy, 1944

That day when we came back from a mission,
in a field beside the tents where we slept
lay a woman and a baby under a blanket.
Beside the blanket was a pile of lira notes.
A line like a chow line snaked through the field.
She was taking them on, one by one,
a squadron of flight crews and ground crews
who could easily get in town whatever they wanted
for a loaf of bread or a pack of cigarettes
but preferred to stand in a muddy field, watching and
    waiting,
while the blanket humped and the woman earned
whatever it was she had to earn in one day from that war.

.

About the Author

Harvey Shapiro's parents came from a rural village outside Kiev, but he became an urban poet, whom Cynthia Ozick has called "*the* American urban poet." Shapiro was born in Chicago and lives in Brooklyn. He has published eight other volumes of poetry. He has worked on magazines and newspapers since 1955, first on *Commentary* and *The New Yorker,* then on *The New York Times Magazine,* of which he was assistant editor from 1964 to 1975, then editor of the *New York Times Book Review* from 1975 to 1983. He is now a deputy editor of the Magazine. He has served on the editorial boards of *Poetry New York* and *Epoch* and received a Rockefeller Foundation grant in poetry in 1967. He has taught English at Cornell and poetry workshops at Columbia and Yale.

Shapiro is a graduate of Yale (B.A. 1947) and of Columbia (M.A. 1948). He was a gunner in a B-17 in the Second World War, receiving the Distinguished Flying Cross and the Air Medal with three oak leaf clusters.

About the Book

National Cold Storage Company was composed on a Mergenthaler Linotron 202 in Sabon with Revue display. Sabon was designed by the late Swiss typographer, teacher, scholar, book designer, and type designer Jan Tschichold.

The book was composed by G & S Typesetters, Inc. in Austin, Texas, and designed by Kachergis Book Design in Pittsboro, North Carolina.

Wesleyan University Press, 1988